Anonymus

Month of Mary for all the Faithful

A Practical Life of the Blessed Virgin

Anonymus

Month of Mary for all the Faithful
A Practical Life of the Blessed Virgin

ISBN/EAN: 9783742814654

Manufactured in Europe, USA, Canada, Australia, Japa

Cover: Foto ©Thomas Meinert / pixelio.de

Manufactured and distributed by brebook publishing software
(www.brebook.com)

Anonymus

Month of Mary for all the Faithful

．

MONTH OF MARY,

FOR ALL THE FAITHFUL;

OR,

A Practical Life of the Blessed Virgin.

FROM THE FRENCH.

" Talis fuit Maria, ut ejus unius vita, omnium sit dis-
ciplina."

Ex libro S. Ambrosii. de Kirginibus.

DUBLIN:

M'GLASHAN & GILL, 50, UPPER SACKVILLE-ST.

1875.

Nihil obstat.

GIRALDUS MOLLOY, S.T.D.,

Censor Theologicus Deputatus.

Imprimatur,

✠ PAUL. CARD. CULLEN,

Archiepiscopus Dublinensis,

Hiberniæ Primas.

APPROBATION

TO THE ORIGINAL FRENCH EDITION.

WE hereby approve of the publication of this work.

Its doctrinal accuracy, the moral reflections, eminently practical, which it contains, and the happy selection of new Examples will, we have no doubt, render this book useful both to the clergy and faithful.

✠ PIERRE HENRI,

Bishop of Belley.

Indulgences granted in favour of those who perform the Devotions of the Month of Mary.

To encourage the faithful to the practice of this beautiful devotion, Pope Pius VII. granted (March 21, 1815) and confirmed for ever (June 18, 1822) the following Indulgences :—To all the faithful who either publicly or in private shall practise some devotion in honour of the Blessed Virgin during the month of May, an Indulgence of 300 days for each day ; and a Plenary Indulgence on any one day of the month on which, after Confession and Communion, they shall pray to God for the wants of the Church. These Indulgences are made applicable by way of suffrage to the suffering souls in Purgatory.

Act of Consecration to the Blessed Virgin.

MOST Holy Virgin, Mother of God, Queen of heaven and earth, Masterpiece of the hands of the Omnipotent, fitting object of the complacency of the Adorable Trinity, perfect model of all virtues; suffer me, at this time of special grace and devotion, to offer thee the tribute of my gratitude and love. Would that I could offer thee the hearts of all mankind; would that I could render thee such homage as the angels and saints shall render thee eternally in heaven; but, since I cannot do so, accept at least the offering which I now make thee of myself. I offer and consecrate to thee my body, my soul, my senses, my faculties, and my life. I recognise and choose thee for my Queen, my Patron, my Protectress, and my Mother. After my God and Saviour, I desire to belong to thee and live for thee alone. It shall ever be my glory to be of the number of thy most faithful servants and most docile and devoted children. Yes, O Mary, after Jesus, in thee do I place my trust, to thee shall I have recourse in all my necessities. Thou shalt be my strength in danger, my refuge in tribulations, my support in sorrow, my guide and model in virtue. I will study to imitate thy humility, sweetness, patience, resignation, modesty, purity, thy love of thy neighbour, and, most of all, thy love of God. These are my resolutions; but, alas! thou knowest my frailty and inconstancy; thou knowest the dangers that surround me, and the enemies that assail me on all sides. O Mother of goodness and mercy! remove the obstacles that impede me in the paths of virtue; help and direct me amidst the thousand perils to which I am exposed; if I stray, recall me; if I fail in courage, strengthen me; if I am called to the conflict, sustain me. But, above all, oh, do not forsake me at the terrible moment that shall decide my lot for eternity; be with me at the hour of death. Then, most of all, be my refuge, my strength and support; defend me from the last and redoubled assaults of the devil; obtain for me courage against the fear of death and the terrors of judgment. And when my soul shall quit this life, receive it into thy maternal arms, and accompany it to the judgment seat of God; obtain for me grace and mercy, and conduct me to heaven, where I shall praise, bless, and love thee for eternity with the angels and saints. Amen.

PREFACE.

WHY this new *Month of Mary?* Is it that there is a dearth of books of this kind? On the contrary there are a great many; but some of them, having been written a long time back, have begun to lose their interest from being too well known; others are meant for only a special class of readers. It has occurred, therefore, to us that a new *Month of Mary* intended for the faithful generally would be of some use, and that is what we have here attempted.

In most of the *Months of Mary* the lecture is divided into three points, with a short moral reflection at the end of each point. This method, so suitable for pious persons who are accustomed to meditation, appears to us to present the inconvenience of not giving sufficient prominence to the moral deduction, of not impressing it enough, and therefore not bringing it fully home to the minds of the ordinary faithful. We have given for each day of the month one only point for consideration, either on the life or the virtues of the Blessed Virgin, with a moral reflection somewhat developed. After that an Example, as much as possible suited to the lecture; and, finally, a little Practice, which recalls in a few words the subject of the meditation, and of which it should be, as it were, the fruit.

Such is the end, such the plan, of this little work. That it may be found useful to souls is the only ambition of the Author.

CONTENTS.

8 CONTENTS.

MONTH OF MARY.

HERE are three principal motives to excite our devotion to the Blessed Virgin, namely, her eminent dignity, the example of the saints, and our own advantage.

1. After God, the object most worthy of our devotion is the glorious Virgin Mary. Enriched from the first moment of her existence with the most precious favours, she is the most holy and perfect of creatures, the masterpiece of the Almighty Creator, the queen of heaven and earth, the sovereign dispensatrix of God's graces, and, what surpasses all her other prerogatives and elevates her far above all other created beings, she is the Mother of God. Such are the titles which this august queen has to our respect and veneration. Oh, how

2

interest herself in behalf of those who are
solicitous to honour her, to love and serve
her! No one ever invoked her, says St.
Bernard, without experiencing the effect
of her tender mercy. Heaven and earth
shall perish, says the holy Louis de Blois,
sooner than she shall fail to succour those
who sincerely invoke her. Her ear is ever
attentive to our prayers; her maternal heart
is ever accessible to our miseries and
moved by our wants, she knows to what
danger we are exposed, she knows also our
weakness; she sees how the devil assails us,
the snares he lays for us, and the efforts he
makes in order to ruin us and drag us into
the abyss, and she is ever ready to aid us
in overcoming those dangers if we only
implore her assistance. Let us then cast
ourselves with confidence into the arms of
this tender mother, invoking her in all
trials and temptations, and laying all our
wants before her, and she will console us
in our miseries and fortify us against our
own weakness and the dangers by which
we are surrounded. Are we in sin? let us
pray to her to obtain pardon for us and she
will speedily reconcile us with her Divine
Son; are we in the state of grace? let us

appeal through her for perseverance, and
we shall be strengthened in our good resolutions and fortified in the paths of justice
and sanctity; in fine, if we be faithful in
honouring Mary, in loving and serving her,
she will guide us in safety to the haven
of a happy eternity, for it is impossible,
say the Holy Fathers, that a true, devoted
servant of Mary should be lost.

EXAMPLE.

A girl of five years of age had her hand dread-
fully bruised by a door; the mother at once took
her to a skilful surgeon, but, notwithstanding
every care and remedy, the wound became rapidly
worse, so that every hope of cure was at an end,
and nothing remained but to amputate the member
in order to save the life of the child. The physician in making this announcement to the mother
told her that the operation need not take place for
three days, but after that time there could not be
further delay. Returning home full of sadness at
this decision, the mother met a pious woman to
whom she related her sad story. "Why do you
abandon yourself to despair?" said this holy soul.
"Go to the Blessed Virgin; throw yourself at her
feet; pray to her with faith, confidence, and perseverance, and you shall certainly obtain the cure
you wish for." Reassured by these words, the
mother and child took courage; they hastened to
an altar of our Blessed Lady, there they prostrated

themselves in prayer, beseeching and conjuring her with tears to hear their prayers and grant their petition. At the end of half an hour, the child suddenly exclaimed, "Mother, I think I am cured." The mother precipitately arose, took the child, and at the door of the church removed the bandages. The hand was perfectly restored, and as well as if the accident had never happened. Beside herself with joy, she related to everyone she met the miracle which the Blessed Virgin had performed. On the day appointed she took her child to the physician. "Well, my good woman," he said, "I see you have decided on having the operation performed." With a joyful countenance she showed him her child's hand, and related to him what had happened. "Ah," said the doctor, who was a man of strong faith, "I am no longer astonished at your daughter's cure, for the Blessed Virgin is a better physician than the whole of us together" (*Rosier de Marie*).

PRACTICE.

Let us form the resolution to honour, love, and serve the Blessed Virgin, not only during this sweet month, but also during our whole life, that we may thereby come to love, praise, and bless her for all eternity in heaven.

FIRST DAY.

BIRTH OF THE BLESSED VIRGIN.

THE Blessed Virgin was born at Nazareth, a little town in Galilee. Her parents were St. Joachim and St. Anne. Tradition says that her parents, who were already stricken in years, had made a promise to the Lord to consecrate their child in an especial manner to His service, should He hear their prayers, by sending them one. Moved by their faith and piety, the Lord granted their petition, and on the 8th of September was born at Nazareth the child who had been destined from all eternity to be the mother of the Saviour.

The birth of Mary had been predicted and announced from the beginning of the world. Scarcely had our first parents been seduced by the infernal serpent, when God, addressing the tempter, said, "Because thou hast deceived the woman, thou art accursed amongst the beasts of the earth; upon thy breast thou shalt go, and earth shalt thou eat all the days of thy life; I will put enmity between thee and the woman, and thy

of which we stand in need. Oh, how happy
has been our lot compared to that of so
many poor infidels who know not God, or
so many heretics whose misfortune it has
been to have been born and reared outside
the Church! How many graces and means
of sanctification have we at our command,
of which they are deprived? But so much
the more culpable shall we be, and the more
severe our punishment if we abuse these
precious favours by not turning them to
good account. Jesus Himself tells us so in
the Gospel; He will insist on more from
him to whom much has been given. Let
us make good use of the means of sanctification which God in His goodness has so
abundantly placed at our command, so that
they may not be to us hereafter a subject
of greater condemnation, but rather of merit
and reward.

EXAMPLE.

*St. Teresa, whilst yet a child, takes the Blessed
Virgin as her mother.*

There lived in Spain, in the 16th century, a saint
renowned for her sublime revelations, the heroism
of her virtues, and the incredible labours she underwent in order to extend the Order of Carmel. of

which she was the reformer. At the age of twelve she had the misfortune to lose her mother, a lady of eminent piety, and to whom she was tenderly attached. Fully conscious of her great loss, the little Teresa, drowned in tears, cast herself before an image of the Blessed Virgin. "Sweet Queen of Heaven," she said, "the loving mother whom I have lost always told me that you never abandon the orphan. Oh! since I now am one show yourself my mother. I will be an obedient and dutiful child to you, I will ever love you with my whole heart." After this prayer, Teresa arose with a more tranquil mind, shedding less bitter tears. From that moment she always evinced towards her heavenly mother all the love and affectionate respect of a dutiful child, and Mary, on her part, constantly treated her as a child of special predilection. Without doubt, it was owing to the protection of this powerful mother that she was indebted for the high degree of sanctity, which has made her one of the most illustrious heroines of the Church; it was through the care of Mary that this *Rose of Carmel* bloomed so brightly and shed so delicious a perfume in the garden of the celestial spouse. "It has always been the case with me," St. Teresa used constantly to say, "that I was sure to get assistance whenever I recommended anything to the Blessed Mother of God" (*Mois de Marie de la Jeunesse Cretienne*).

PRACTICE.

Let us thank God for having caused us to be born in the bosom of the true Church, preferably

to so many others; for having shed upon us the
light of faith, and instructed us in the saving truths
of the Gospel. What a terrible account shall ours
be, if we abuse these graces by failing to profit by
them?

SECOND DAY.

THE GRACES WHICH ACCOMPANIED THE BIRTH OF THE BLESSED VIRGIN.

THOUGH there was no external circumstance
to mark, as an extraordinary event, the
birth of the Blessed Virgin, yet there was
in reality much to distinguish it from all
others. It is of faith that all men are conceived and born with the stain of original
sin attached to them; but by a special
privilege, bestowed on her alone, Mary
was exempt from this sad consequence of
the fall of our first parents. From the
first moment of her existence she was all
pure, all holy, and immaculate. God, who
had destined her to become the Mother of
His Son, would not have her to be, for even
an instant, under the anathema of sin and
the consequent dominion of the demon. And,
indeed, as she was to give to the world the

God of all sanctity, it was not meet that
she should have been previously sullied by
sin; as she was to subvert the throne of
Satan by crushing the head of the infernal
serpent, it was not fitting that Satan should
have at any time, established his empire in
her heart.   The Mother of God was, therefore, created in the state of justice and
sanctity in which our first parents were
created, and from which they fell,—in that
state of purity and innocence in which the
angels were called into existence.   Of
Mary alone, of all creatures, it could with
truth be said : Thou art all beautiful, and
there is no stain in thee.

The Council of Trent, when declaring
that all men were born subject to original
sin, distinctly declares that this decision
does not apply to the blessed and immaculate Mother of God.   Finally, to set the
question for ever at rest, the Sovereign
Pontiff, speaking in the name of the infal-
lible Church of God, on the 8th of December,
1854, pronounced a solemn decision, making
the doctrine of the Immaculate Conception
of the Blessed Virgin an article of faith.
But, not only was Mary preserved from
original sin, she, moreover, had bestowed

upon her in the first moment of her existence, an abundance of most precious graces.
God wished to render her worthy of His
Son to whom she was to give birth, and for
that end enriched her with all the gifts of
the Holy Spirit. He conferred upon her
every perfection which a creature is capable
of receiving; He raised her above all the
celestial intelligences; He made her more
beautiful than the angels, purer than the
seraphim, so that of Mary, and of her alone,
it can be said that, even at her birth, she
surpassed in grace and perfection all the
angels and saints. How different our birth
from that of Mary! Conceived in sin, we
were born in enmity with our God; heaven
was shut against us. But the Lord, ever
good and merciful, quickly freed us from
that unhappy state by admitting us into
the number of His friends and adopted
children. Scarcely had we seen the light
when we were carried to the baptismal
font, and there, as soon as the blessed water
flowed upon our brow, divine grace flowed
into our soul, and we became regenerated,
cleansed, sanctified; original sin was washed
away, we received a new birth, we became
new creatures; from being enemies of

God, we became His friends; from being children of wrath and malediction, we became children of grace and love; from being exiles from the kingdom of God, we became heirs to heaven, brethren to Jesus Christ, and entitled to a participation in His eternal glory hereafter. The graces of Baptism not only effaced in us the stain of original sin, and restored to us all the rights and titles of which its commission had deprived us, it also enriched us with the gifts of the Holy Ghost, it planted in our soul the virtues of Faith, Hope, and Charity; it purified us in the adorable blood of Jesus Christ, and we came forth from that saving bath as pure and bright as the angels. How manifold and precious the graces bestowed on us in bap ism! How solemn the promises and stringent the obligations we contracted by it! We there and then bound ourselves to live according to the maxims of the Gospel and the example of Jesus Christ. How have we fulfilled these engagements? Oh, if we have had the misfortune to break them, let us bemoan our unfaithfulness before God, petitioning Him for pardon, and making the firm resolution to lead henceforth a life more regular, more Christian, and more in conformity with our baptismal engagements.

EXAMPLE.

Devotion of Marius Olive to the Blessed Virgin.

The life of this young man affords an illustrious example of tender devotion to the Blessed Virgin. He was born at Marseilles on the Octave of the Assumption, and received in baptism the name of Marius in honour of Mary, in accordance with the pious wish of his parents. Some days after they brought the infant to a celebrated chapel dedicated to the Blessed Virgin, under the title of *Notre Dame de la Garde*, to offer him solemnly to his august patroness. His life showed how agreeable the offering was to Mary. From the very first there was noticeable in him a tender devotion for his *good mother*, the name he always addressed her by from the time he could first lisp it. A statue or picture of Mary had the greatest attraction for him, and he recognised them at the most considerable distance; "See," he used to say, "see my good mother!" Scarcely was he three years old when he was invested with the holy scapular, the little devotions attached to which were performed for him until he was sufficiently old to repeat them himself. His love for Mary increased with his years; at fourteen, he felt great delight in joining the Confraternity of the Blessed Virgin, established in the Seminary of Aix, and he was a model for all the associates by his filial love for Mary. He had recourse to her in all his doubts and perplexities; later on he consulted her regarding his vocation. Assured that God called him to the priesthood, he adjured his holy patroness to confirm him in this resolution, and when his mother objected to his delicacy, his great youth, and the imprudence of forming a precipitate resolution, "Mother," he replied, "I have prayed and got others to pray to the Blessed Virgin, and she has heard me; it is what I ought to do." God was satisfied with his holy intention, and soon after called Marius to Himself. In his last moments, the pious youth redoubled his love and devotion for Mary; he regarded her next to God, as he said to his brother, as the cause of the joy with which his soul was filled. He was constantly occupied with the thought of Jesus and Mary, and when he appeared scarcely to breathe, it was only these sacred names that could attract his attention. When he seemed to suffer from violent temptations, so that all his frame trembled, some one said to him to have confidence in Mary, and immediately he was restored to peace. In these holy sentiments he breathed his last sigh on the Octave of the Annunciation of the Blessed Virgin. After death, his countenance exhibited a marvellous beauty; it was remarked that his body shared already the joy which his blessed soul possessed in the society of that good Mother whom he had so tenderly loved in life (*Mois de Marie, &c., par M. l'Abbé Michaud*).

PRACTICE.

Let us be ever mindful that the chief duty of a Christian is to fulfil the promises made in Baptism.

By these we shall be judged when, hereafter, we appear before the tribunal of God. Wo to us, if we be found wanting in the observance of them!

THIRD DAY.

THE BLESSED VIRGIN RECEIVES THE NAME OF MARY.

SOME days after her birth, the Blessed Virgin received from her parents the name of Mary, a name expressive, at the same time, of her greatness and power, of sweetness and goodness. In truth, the name of Mary signifies august sovereign; it signifies also star of the sea, and the Blessed Virgin fulfils to the utmost all that is indicated by this mystical name. She is the sovereign of angels and men, the queen of heaven and earth, she is also our star; she is, according to St. Bernard, that brilliant star which safely guides us through the thousand perils by which we are menaced on the troubled ocean of this life; she is the benign star by which we securely steer into the harbour of salvation. The name of Mary is a subject of happiness and joy to

heaven! Such is the power and efficacy of
the holy name of Mary, says a learned
author, that when it is pronounced, all
heaven rejoices and the angels are filled
with delight. The name of Mary is a
source of hope and consolation on earth.
After the adorable name of Jesus, there is
no other that can impart to us so much
consolation or inspire us with such confidence as that of Mary. Witness with
what earnestness those who are in sorrow
and affliction press round the altar of this
august sovereign. Thither the sinner goes
to bewail his crimes, the weak frail Christian to seek for succour; there the heart
plunged in grief and disappointment goes
to obtain patience and consolation. The
name of Mary is also a source of fear and
terror to hell. Oh, how the devils tremble
and are seized with terror at the sole mention of the name of Mary, says St. Bernard.
The name of Mary is so terrible to the
demons, says, again, St. Bonaventure, that
when we invoke it, the evil spirits are
driven away in dismay. We find all the
saints and sacred writers unanimous in
making use of similar expressions; they all
agree in assuring us of the efficacy of this

sacred name in putting to flight the spirit
of darkness. Finally, the name of Mary is
a source of peace and salvation to those who
invoke it with confidence. After that of
Jesus, no other name has such potency in
heaven as that of His holy Mother; none,
therefore, after His divine name, which can
obtain for us so much grace and assistance.
However miserable we may be, how deeply
soever we have sinned, we should never
despair; we can do all things through
Mary, provided we invoke her with confidence. O you, whoever you may be, exclaims St. Bernard, who are tossed on the
boisterous sea of this world, would you
avoid miserable shipwreck? look to Mary.
Are you exposed to violent temptations and
wish to overcome them? turn to Mary.
Does the fear of God's judgment and the
magnitude of your sins fill you with sadness,
and despondency tempt you to despair? call
upon Mary. In doubts, in danger, in grief
and adversities, think of Mary, invoke Mary.
May this holy name be ever in your
mouth and in your heart! Following Mary
you shall not stray, praying to her you
shall never give way to despair; if she
support you, you shall not fall; if she protect

you, you shall have nothing to fear; if she be propitious you shall attain the harbour of salvation.

EXAMPLE.

Holy death obtained through devotion to Mary.

Pére de Smet, a famous missioner of the Society of Jesus amongst the savage tribes of America, some years ago arrived at a colony of the Pottowatomies, situated on the Osage river; whilst the cargo was being discharged, they carried on board a young man who was dangerously ill. It was already late in the day, and on account of his luggage, the missionary could not take up his quarters in the wigwam, which the chief had prepared for his reception. He, therefore, remained on board. During the night the young man suffered very much. His groans attracted Pére de Smet, and brought him to his bedside to soothe and console him. These charitable attentions of the missionary touched the young man, and led him to open his heart to him. "I am a Catholic," he said, "and I have received a thoroughly religious education from an uncle who is a zealous ecclesiastic. I have remembered and put in practice his holy instructions, and especially I have ever had a great devotion to the Mother of God. I have sojourned these six years past in the mountains amongst a savage tribe without once having met with a priest, yet I have never been forgetful of my heavenly Mother, Mary." "Without doubt, it is she who has sent me to you at this time of danger," said the venerable missionary; and she means to verify in your regard the words of St. Bernard, that no one who had recourse to her was ever abandoned. Believe me it is so; profit, therefore, by the grace which she has obtained for you. · It is a long time since you have purified your conscience; perhaps there are many things with which it reproaches you. Begin your confession." The young man gladly availed himself of the invitation of the minister of God; he confessed with sentiments of the greatest piety, and received the last sacraments. Père de Smet learned afterwards that he died the day after he reached the end of his journey (*Annales de la Propagation de la Foi*).

PRACTICE.

Let us frequently call upon the holy name of Mary, particularly in times of temptation. In those moments of dreadful danger, let us throw ourselves into the arms of this most tender Mother. She is sure to come to our aid, she will effectually protect us, and make us triumph over the enemies of our salvation.

———

FOURTH DAY.

PRESENTATION OF THE BLESSED VIRGIN IN THE TEMPLE.

WHEN Mary was but three years old, her parents took her with them to the Temple of Je-

rusalem, and there they presented her to
the Lord in accordance with their previous
promise, and solemnly and publicly devoted
her wholly to His service. The Church
celebrates the Presentation of the Blessed
Virgin on the 21st November. What
thoughts and sentiments filled the soul of
Mary whilst her parents thus offered her
to God at the foot of His altar? By what·
close ties did she not unite herself to her
Creator and her God! The Holy Ghost
has not revealed to us what passed in the
heart of Mary on this occasion, but all
tradition and authority agree in saying that
she then consecrated herself to the Lord in
an absolute and irrevocable manner. She
consecrated to Him her heart, her soul, her
body, all her faculties; she devoted herself to Him entirely and for ever. She
made a renunciation of her will, her goods,
her family, all that she possessed most dear
and precious, to give herself to God without
reserve. Nothing daunted her in making
this sacrifice, neither extreme youth, nor
love of parents, nor the complete seclusion
to which it consigned her, nor the austere
and penitential life which it involved ; she
readily and unhesitatingly made an offering

of all for the salvation of her soul. What
wonderful devotedness and heroic virtue in
a child of three years old ! The fathers of
the Church have ever regarded the consecration of the Blessed Virgin in the Temple
as the most perfect sacrifice and most
pleasing act of religion ever made to God
from the beginning of the world until
then.

How much does the Presentation of the
Blessed Virgin condemn our love of our own
ease and sloth in the service of God! Mary
consecrated herself to the Lord from her
most tender infancy, and as soon as she was
capable of knowing and loving Him ; and
we are ever finding a pretext to postpone
and evade those duties which we owe to
God and our immortal souls. In vain does
grace knock at the door of our heart, we
resist it; in vain does the Lord urge us to
devote ourselves to His service, we reject
His tender invitations ; in vain does remorse
agitate and alarm us, we seek in dissipation
of thought to escape the reproaches of conscience, and continue to live a life of
sloth and negligence, even, perhaps, of sin.
Mary consecrated herself to God irrevocably
and without reserve ; having once given

herself to Him, she served him with fidelity,
and made continual progress in virtue; she
became each day more fervent, more pious,
more inflamed with the love of God. How
far, alas! are we from imitating her constancy! What has our life been but a
continued succession of promises and with-
drawal from those engagements; of resolutions to be better, and relapses into sin. We
sue to God for pardon, promising to be
henceforth faithful, never to offend Him
again, yet how often, perhaps, even in a
day or two, have we fallen back into those
very faults which we affected to detest with
our whole heart. Mary made an unreserved
consecration of herself to God; she offered
to Him her heart with all its affections, and
her soul with all its aspirations. Has our
offering of ourself been after this manner?
Is it thus we devote ourselves to God?
Do we offer Him a heart free from all guilty
attachments and exempt from all culpable
affections to sin? God cannot dwell in a
divided soul, in a heart of which vice and
passion hold possession. In imitation of
Blessed Mary, let us now consecrate ourselves to God without delay, offering to
Him, sincerely and unreservedly, all that

that Jesus Christ Himself has said in His Gospel,
The kingdom of God suffereth violence, and the
violent bear it away.

———

FIFTH DAY.

THE BLESSED VIRGIN PASSES HER YOUTH IN THE TEMPLE.

AN ancient tradition, founded on Sacred
Scripture, informs us that one portion of
the Temple was assigned to young virgins
who dwelt there in retreat and recollection.
Wise and holy matrons watched over them;
instructed and directed them; taught them
to read and meditate upon the holy Scriptures; and especially trained them in the
love and practice of virtue.   Amongst these
young virgins Mary was placed when she
was presented in the Temple at the age of
three years.   There she was reared up in the
fear and love of God, there she spent the hap-
piest days of her life. Apart from the world,
alone with God, she was wholly occupied
about her salvation and perfection.   What
rapid progress did she not make in virtue!
Each day beheld her more humble, more
modest, more pious, more charitable.   Full

of respect for, and submission towards her
superiors, she regarded them as holding the
place of God in her regard, and obeyed
them with eagerness and joy. Mary was
also full of sweetness and kindness towards
her companions; she lived in perfect unity
and peace with them; she bore with their
peculiarities and defects; she consoled them
in their troubles, assisted them in their needs,
and rendered them every kind of good service.
Mary edified every one by the holiness of her
actions and the regularity of her conduct;
she was the first at every duty, the most
exact in observing the law of God, the most
deeply grounded in humility, the most perfect in the practice of the other virtues.
Such was the good example that Mary constantly gave during her sojourn in the
Temple.

Mary was also most assiduous in prayer;
with it she commenced and ended each day;
and she prayed also frequently during the day.
"She spoke little," says St. Ambrose, "but
she meditated much." "She had attained
to such a habit of mental prayer," says the
same father, "that nothing could trouble
or interrupt her in this holy exercise. In
prayer she found her greatest happiness

and sweetest consolation; but, then, with
what faith, with what confidence and love
did she pray! Ever united to God in heart
and mind, she dwelt continually in His
divine presence. To Him she directed all
her thoughts, words, and actions, so that
Mary's life in the Temple may be said to
have been a continual prayer."

Let us imitate the virtues which Mary
practised in the Temple. Like her, let us
respect those who are placed over us, and
who have a right to command us; being
always submissive and obedient to them.
Let us recollect that they derive their
authority from God, and that to fail in
respect and submission towards those in
authority over us, is to fail in respect and
submission towards God Himself. Like
Mary, let us be kind, patient, and charitable towards our neighbour, avoiding what
would give them pain, bearing with their
defects, seeking opportunities of rendering
them kind services, compassionating and
comforting them in times of trial, and doing
all for them that we would have them do
for us. Finally, let us, like Mary, direct
all our actions to God by prayer,—praying
the commencement of the day, to offer

it to God and to ask the grace to spend it
holily; praying at night, to thank God for
the favours He has conferred on us, and to
sue for pardon for such faults as we have
been guilty of; praying also and raising
our hearts to God from time to time during
the day, offering Him our trials, our labours,
all our actions. Thus devoted to God and
sanctified by prayer, our life will flow on
full of good works and merits in the sight
of heaven.

EXAMPLE.

Imitation of the Blessed Virgin.

Like all children of predestination, Leonie R——
had a great devotion to the Blessed Virgin from
the most tender years. Whilst yet a child, her
mother happening to tell her how the Blessed
Virgin was consecrated to God in the Temple at
three years of age, she promptly exclaimed, "and
I also will give myself to God like the Blessed
Virgin." "But," the mother replied, "the Blessed
Virgin whilst in the Temple, practised patience,
sweetness, and humility; she bore with the way-
wardness of her companions; she showed no dis-
inclination to do what she was commanded, but
always obeyed promptly and without a murmur;
you often act quite differently from all this."
"Well, I will amend," replied the child. " The
Blessed Virgin when in the Temple," the mother

said again, "loved God with her whole heart, and offered to Him all her thoughts and actions." "I will also love Him like her," replied Leonie. "The Blessed Virgin devoted herself to prayer," added the mother; "she prayed in the morning, in the evening, and frequently during the day, and her prayers were always full of fervour, piety, and recollection." "Teach me a prayer," said the child, "and I will offer it to God and the Blessed Virgin every day." The prayer was soon supplied, and Leonie never let a single day pass that she did not repeat it with a singular devotion. According as this child of benediction advanced in years so also the more fervent did she become in labouring for her salvation and perfection, and the more closely did she study to imitate the virtues of her whom she had chosen as her model. Her ejaculatory prayers to Mary were almost continual; she had recourse to her in all circumstances with the most filial confidence. It gave her the truest delight when she had the opportunity of doing something in honour of her heavenly Mother; she adorned her chapel, decorated her altars, and in every way in her power gave proof of the love for her with which she abounded. And not only her childhood, but still more her youth, did she consecrate to Mary, passing her entire life in her love and that of her Divine Son. Like so many souls specially dear to God, she was early called to her never-ending reward. Being made perfect in a short time, her soul pleased God, and, therefore, He hastened to bring her out of the midst of an iniquitous world, lest its wickedness should alter her understanding, or its deceit beguile her soul.

As her end drew nigh she placed the last days of her life under the protection of her whom she had always served as a mother. She passed some days in a retreat consecrated to Mary, where she meditated on the years that shall never end, and commended herself and the terrible passage from earth to eternity to the care of her whom the dying have never invoked in vain. Mary heard the prayer of her beloved child. Leonie came forth from her sweet and happy retreat enjoying a profound peace and a spirit of entire resignation to the holy will of God; and though she was but twenty-seven years of age, she saw death approach without fear and without regret. She fell asleep calmly in the arms of Mary, as a child on the bosom of its mother. Oh, how happy is the death of those who have spent their lives in the love, and service, and imitation of the Blessed Virgin! (*Mois de Marie de la Jeunesse Chretienne*).

PRACTICE.

Imitate the conduct of Mary in the Temple; like her be submissive and obedient to your superiors, kind and charitable to your neighbours, pious and recollected in your prayers, and faithful and exact in all your duties.

SIXTH DAY.

THE BLESSED VIRGIN IS CONFIDED TO THE CARE OF ST. JOSEPH.

THE Blessed Virgin was not more than eight or nine years old, and leading a life in the Temple that was the admiration of angels and men by its holiness and shining virtues, when she had the misfortune to lose her father, St. Joachim, and, shortly after, her mother, St. Anne. This double affliction was a great grief to her, for Mary, like all wise and virtuous children, tenderly loved her parents. What tears did she not shed at the feet of the Lord! There she came to lay down the burden of her trials and her sorrows; there she poured out her heart in sweet and fervent prayers. Happy they who, like Mary, come to shed their tears on the bosom of God and at the foot of His altar! They will find there the only consolation that can soothe their misfortunes by aiding them to bear them with holy resignation. It is the common belief that the Blessed Virgin remained in the Temple up to the age of fourteen or fifteen; poor

orphan that she was, without help or
means, what was there to tempt her from
this holy retreat? The Lord, who never
forsakes those who serve Him faithfully,
did not abandon her; she was confided to
one who was her kinsman, a venerable old
man named Joseph. He was a poor artizan,
a carpenter by trade, but a man of great
piety and consummate virtue; he was the
holiest and most perfect of men; and it was
by reason of his saintly qualities and eminent
virtues that he merited to be chosen the
protector and supporter of Mary. In truth,
the moment drew near when, without
ceasing to be a virgin, Mary was to bring
to the world the Saviour of mankind; she
therefore had need of a protector, one, who
by his labour should furnish support to
Mary and her Divine Son, and St. Joseph
was chosen to fulfil these exalted functions.
What a glorious employment was that of
St. Joseph; how happy it must have been
to him to be associated with the purest
of virgins in watching over the infancy of
Jesus! with what zeal and fidelity he
acquitted himself of these sacred duties!
Penetrated with the deepest reverence for
the Divine Infant, he bestowed an unceas-

...ng care upon them, he rescued Him from the fury of Herod, he nourished Him by the labour of his own hands, he loved Him as his adopted child, and adored Him as his Saviour and his God.   St. Joseph was also full of veneration and respect for Mary; he rendered her every kind service in his power, assisted her by his wise counsels, consoled her in her anxieties and troubles, and was the faithful companion of her journeys; he was to her at once a guardian, a protector, and a father.

It was by faithfully fulfilling the duties of his state of life that St. Joseph was sanctified. It is in the same manner that we are to attain to sanctity.   Whatever be our state or condition in life, we all have duties to fulfil, duties that are of strict obligation ; and it is mainly through the faithful ful- filment of these duties that we can hope to accomplish our salvation.   Are we, like St. Joseph, placed in charge of a family ?   Let us be solicitous for those who are committed to our care, watching over them, correcting them when they do wrong, giving them good example by our words, our acts, our whole conduct.   Let us recollect that when we come to be judged, we shall have to

answer to God, not only with regard to the
salvation of our own soul, but also for the
salvation of all those who have been confided
to us; and wo to us if one single soul
perish through our negligence! We shall
have to account to God soul for soul. Are
we, on the other hand, placed under a superior, or a master, and bound to obey and
be submissive to the will of others; let us
not murmur or be impatient at our lot; let
us bear in mind that Jesus Christ Himself,
all God as He was, willed to be in subjection and to obey others during His life on
earth. I am come, He says, not to do my
own will but the will of God the Father
who sent me; I am come, not to be served
but to serve. How should not the example
of Jesus Christ teach us to bear with resignation, and even with joy all that may be
painful or irksome in obeying those who
are in authority over us! Finally, in whatever position we are placed by divine
providence, let us fulfil the duties of our
state of life with fidelity, in a spirit of faith,
and under the eye of God, and we will thus
become, like St. Joseph, perfect Christians
and great saints.

EXAMPLE.

Pious Pilgrimage and Cure.

A devout female named Marie Françoise Petitot, of the diocese of Besançon, was deprived of the use of her limbs for thirty-three years; they were completely paralyzed and contracted under her. She had consulted the most skilful physicians and had tried every remedy without effect. Despairing of help from human means, she determined to have recourse to heaven. As she had a great confidence in the Blessed Virgin, she formed the resolution to make a pilgrimage to the shrine of Notre Dame des Eremites in Switzerland, and begged her parents to take her there, but they constantly refused to do so, saying the expense would be only money thrown away, and that God would not perform a miracle in her favour. On the approach of May, 1850, she redoubled her importunity and prayers. At last a poor woman remarking her great faith in the mother of God, offered to bring her in a poor vehicle which she had. After seven days of toil and privations they arrived at Notre Dame des Eremites on the evening of the 18th of May. Next day, which was the Feast of Pentecost, the poor cripple had herself carried before the miraculous image of the Blessed Virgin. It was at the time when the solemn Mass was about to be celebrated, at which she assisted with a piety full of faith and confidence, and was praying with great fervour, when all at once, during the Elevation, she felt a thrill run through her

whole body, and at the same moment the full us,
of her limbs was restored to her. The late invalid
raised herself to her knees, shedding tears of
gratitude and joy. A great commotion quickly
took place amongst the congregation, every one
rushing forward to witness the miracle. A charitable lady gave stockings to the girl, who put them
on for the first time for upwards of thirty years,
and forthwith approached the Holy Table. After
Mass she returned to her lodging on foot. She remained three days more at Notre Dame des Eremites,.
and each day went to and returned from the church
on foot, surrounded by a crowd of persons who
were attracted by the report of the miracle. A
formal report of the cure was drawn up and for-
warded to her native parish, but the fame of it had
already reached it ; and when she re-entered France
her progress had quite the character of a triumphal
procession in honour of Mary. Many flocked from
all sides to see her, and wonder at her cure ; and
many, in consequence, who had been unbelievers
or neglectful of their religious duties, were converted.—(*Extract from l'Union Francomtoise, 13th
June,* 1850.)

PRACTICE.

In whatever condition Providence has placed
you, never repine at your lot, but apply yourself
to the faithful fulfilment of the duties of your state
of life, bearing with patience the trials and misfortunes you may meet with, and offering them to
God in atonement for your sins; thus will you
succeed in sanctifying and saving your soul.

SEVENTH DAY.

THE BLESSED VIRGIN CHOSEN TO BE THE MOTHER OF GOD.

AFTER spending, according to the tradition, eleven or twelve years in the Temple, Mary quitted that happy retreat and went with St. Joseph to reside at Nazareth. She there lived in the most complete retirement, and in the practice of every virtue. In common with every pious member of the race of Israel, she sighed and prayed without ceasing for the coming of the Messiah; but, at the same time, she was very far from thinking of herself as the Mother of God the Saviour. Never had she an idea that the Lord would raise her to so sublime a dignity—one of which she held herself wholly unworthy. But God, who loves to unite Himself to the humble, and heaps His benefits on them, had already chosen her in preference to all other creatures, and accordingly He sent one of those happy spirits that surround His throne to announce to her that she was to become the Mother of the Redeemer promised and expected during so

many ages. Mary was alone in her place
of retreat, and probably engaged in prayer,
says St. Bernard, when of a sudden the
Angel Gabriel presented himself before her,
and addressed her in these words—"Hail,
full of grace; the Lord is with thee; blessed
art thou amongst women." Never before
had human creature been addressed in terms
of praise like to these. Mary, profoundly
humble, was only troubled and alarmed by
them; she knew not what to think or believe about what she heard and saw. The
Angel, seeing her troubled, hastened to re-
assure her—"Fear not, Mary," he said,
" thou hast found grace with God. Behold
thou shalt conceive and bear a Son, and
thou shalt call His name Jesus. He shall be
great and shall be called the Son of the Most
High, and the Lord God shall give unto
Him the throne of David His Father, and
He shall reign in the House of Jacob for
ever, and of His kingdom there shall be no
end." These words dissipated Mary's first
cause of trouble, but at the same time led
to a new disquietude. And Mary said to
the Angel—How shall this be accomplished in me, as I am resolved to remain
a virgin? Be not disturbed, replied the

Angel, for in becoming a mother you shall
at the same time not cease to be a virgin.
The Child whom you shall bring forth shall
be conceived by the Holy Ghost, who shall
overshadow thee; "and therefore the Holy
which shall be born of thee shall be called
the Son of God." Her apprehensions on
this score being thus removed, Mary cried
out with sentiments of profound submission
and humility—"Behold the handmaid of
the Lord. Be it done to me according to
thy word." The Angel, who awaited only
her consent, immediately disappeared, and
returned to heaven, having fulfilled his
mission. But at the moment—O ineffable
prodigy !—the greatest and most wonderful
of mysteries took place in Mary. The
Eternal Word, the only Son of God, descended into her chaste womb, there to take
to Himself a body and soul like to ours,
there to become truly man, without ceasing
to be God; and Mary became mother without ceasing to be a virgin. Thus was accomplished for our salvation the adorable
mystery of the Incarnation, and thus also
the most humble of virgins was raised to
the sublime dignity of Mother of God.

In the Holy Communion we have the hap-

piness of receiving the same God whom Mary
received at the moment of His Incarnation.
As often as we approach the Holy Table we
truly receive into our breast this same Jesus,
whom Mary bore in her womb. We receive
His Body, His Blood, His Soul, His Divinity. His Body then becomes our food,
His Blood our drink. His Soul communi-
cates to us Its strength and sanctity; His
Divinity raises us so as to become as it were
like unto God. The union we contract
with Jesus Christ is so close and intimate
that we become as it were one with Him.
As the food which we take changes into
our own substance, and becomes identified
with us, so by Holy Communion we are
identified with Jesus Christ, so that it is no
longer we who live or act, but it is Jesus
Christ who lives and acts in us—to use the
beautiful expression of the Apostle—O
wonderful, ineffable union! And not only
does the Holy Communion unite us inti-
mately with Christ, but it also advances us
in grace and in the spiritual life; it pre-
serves and confirms us in virtue; it gives
us strength and courage to resist temptations
and to repress the evil tendencies that continually solicit us to sin. Let us, therefore,

often approach to this august Sacrament, bringing to it a pure heart, profound humility, a lively faith, a tender confidence, and above all an ardent love; for Jesus, who makes it His delight to dwell with the children of men, earnestly desires to come into our soul to load it with His choicest and most precious graces.

EXAMPLE.

A Child preserved from the Flames.

In the early ages of the Church it was the custom to give to little children who still preserved their baptismal innocence the co: secr ited particles which remained after the Communion of the faithful. It happened one day that a young Jewish child who went to school with little Christian children, went to the church with them and innocently presented himself with the others to receive the particles of the Holy Eucharist. On his return home he related to his father what he had done. The father, who was a brutal man and most envenomed against the Christian religion, got into a sort of frenzy. Being a glass-maker by trade, he seized his unhappy child and cast him alive into the blazing furnace which he used for melting his glass. Shortly after, his mother, who had been absent, returned home, and, knowing nothing of what had passed, she sought her son on every side. As none could give her any information, she traversed the various quarters of the town in search of him, but all in vain. Inconsolable at the loss of her beloved child, she gave way to her grief, calling upon him by name as if he were present. All at once, to her surprise, a voice replied calling her, mother. She was struck with astonishment, and ran to the furnace from whence the voice seemed to proceed; she opened the door and looked in. What was her affright when she saw her poor child amidst the flames, but still alive! She called her neighbours to her aid; everyone hastening in order to witness the prodigy. They drew the child from the fire, safe and sound, and asked him how it was he had fallen into the furnace, and how he had been preserved in the midst of the burning flames. He related how his father had thrown him into it for having assisted at the service of the Christians, but that a great lady, beaming with light, had preserved him from the flames, covering him with her mantle; that she had given him food to appease his hunger, and that she perfectly resembled the image of the Blessed Virgin which he had seen in the church. It was known then that Mary had saved him and preserved his life by defending him from the flames. The Emperor of Constantinople—where the miracle occurred—having been informed of the barbarous conduct of this unnatural father, had him arrested and brought to justice; but the wretch, so far from being converted, became all the more hardened in his infidelity, and died impenitent. As to the mother, she had herself instructed in the Christian faith, received the grace of Baptism, and became one of the most faithful and fervent of Christians (*Evagrius, and Gregory of Tours*).

PRACTICE.

Approach frequently the Sacrament of the Blessed Eucharist; we need it to sustain us and enable us to resist our passions, for we are weak and miserable; but take heed to approach it ever with holy dispositions and a soul all prepared. Make each Communion as if it were your last.

EIGHTH DAY.

THE BLESSED VIRGIN VISITS HER COUSIN ST. ELIZABETH.

No sooner had the Blessed Virgin conceived in her chaste womb the Eternal Word than, animated with the desire of bestowing on the house of Zachary a share of those divine graces with which her soul was filled, she left her peaceful retreat and went into the mountains of Judea to visit her cousin Elizabeth. She went with haste, for charity urged her forward, and "charity brooks no delay," says St. Ambrose. Arrived at the end of her journey, she enters the house of Zachary, salutes Elizabeth, and embraces her; but—miracle of grace!—at the voice

of Mary, the infant of Elizabeth bounds
with joy in the womb of his mother; he is
sanctified on the instant by the presence of
the Saviour. Finally, the grace received by
the infant communicating itself to the
mother, Elizabeth was in turn filled with
the Holy Ghost. Supernaturally enlightened, she at once understood all the wonders
which heaven had wrought in favour of
Mary; and accordingly, full of respect and
admiration for the youthful mother, she
cried out—"Blessed art thou amongst
women, and blessed is the fruit of thy
womb."   Then she immediately added—
"Whence is this to me that the Mother of
my Lord should come to me?   For behold,
as soon as thy salutation sounded in my
ears, the infant in my womb leaped for joy.
And blessed art thou that hast believed, because those things shall be accomplished
that were spoken to thee by the Lord."
Mary then comprehended that Elizabeth
was enlightened regarding the mystery of
the Incarnation, and that it was the Holy
Ghost Himself who had revealed it to her.
No longer able, therefore, to conceal her
august quality of Mother of God, she gave
way to her transports of lively gratitude,

wound charity. Let us respect the name
of Christian which we bear; let us never
make use of a single word that would tend
to violate the virtue of holy purity; let all
our expressions be marked by a holy reserve.
Let us never be unmindful that we are in
the presence of God who hears all our words,
and who will one day demand of us a strict
and rigorous account of them.

EXAMPLE.

The Miraculous Conversion.

M. Alphonse Ratisbonne was born of a rich and
distinguished Jewish family residing at Strasbourg.
Like so many young men who devote themselves
to a life of pleasure, he was devoid of all faith, and
practised no religion.   He had an elder brother,
a convert and a Catholic priest. He had conceived
such an aversion to this brother that he would neither see him nor hold any communication with him.
He fostered a bitter hatred for priests, churches,
religious houses, and especially for the Jesuits, the
sole mention of which Society was enough to put
him in a fury. Towards the close of the year 1841,
previous to his intended marriage with a relative
who was as yet too young, he determined on
making a voyage of pleasure to the East.   He had
an aversion to going to Rome ; but Providence,
that disposes everything to its designs, brought
him there in spite of himself   He there made the

acquaintance of M. Theodore de Bussières, who from having been a Protestant had become a fervent Catholic. M. Bussières spoke to him regarding the Catholic religion, its grandeur and advantages. M. Ratisbonne replied with sarcasm and impiety. "Since you are so strong-minded," said M. de Bussières, "will you have the courage to submit to a harmless test?" "What test?" "That of carrying about you a medal of the Blessed Virgin." M. Ratisbonne laughed and shrugged his shoulders. He, however, accepted the medal, and scoffingly exclaimed, "Behold me now Catholic, apostolic, and Roman!" "But this is not all," said M. de Bussières; "you have to recite every day this prayer in honour of the Blessed Virgin;" and he gave him a copy of the *Memorare* or Prayer of St. Bernard. "Well, agreed; I will do so." It was then the 15th January, 1842. On the night of the 19th or 20th M. Ratisbonne was awakened suddenly, and saw fixed before him a great black cross of a peculiar shape, but without any figure of Christ upon it. In vain did he endeavour to get rid of this cross: on what side soever he turned, there it was again before him. Next day M. de Bussières, who had charge of the obsequies of one of his friends who had died suddenly, asked him to accompany him to the Church of San Andrea, whither he went to make preparation for the funeral service. Not many moments after M. Ratisbonne had entered, when, like St. Paul on his way to Damascus, he was all at once struck by grace. The whole church disappeared from his view; he saw but one thing; he saw before him, all beautiful, brilliant, full of sweetness and majesty, the

Blessed Virgin herself, just as she was represented
on the miraculous medal which he wore about his
neck.   Urged by an irresistible power, he fell upon
his knees and watered the floor with his tears.   An
interior supernatural light illumined his mind;
without ever having studied the Catholic religion,
he found himself acquainted with all its principal
truths.   He saw the unhappy state of his soul
with affright; he saw it stained with original sin,
and earnestly begged the grace of baptism.   It was
administered to him some days later in presence of
an immense number brought together by the report of the miracle.   M. Ratisbonne has since renounced the world, and joined the Jesuits, amongst
whom as a priest he labours for the salvation of
souls.   This extraordinary conversion has been declared miraculous by a decree of the Sovereign
Pontiff (*Extract from Narrative of the Conversion
of M. Ratisbonne*).

PRACTICE.

Be ever most reserved and prudent in your dis-
course; never say a word that would scandalize
your neighbour.   What a misfortune were we by
sinful language to cause a soul to sin and be eternally lost!   Through all eternity that soul would
continue to accuse us, to curse and invoke vengeance upon us.

NINTH DAY.

JOURNEY OF THE BLESSED VIRGIN TO BETH-
LEHEM, AND BIRTH OF JESUS.

THE time of the birth of the Saviour was
at hand when the Emperor Cæsar Augustus,
who then possessed the empire of the whole
world, ordered a general census of his kingdom. Cyrinus, the governor of Syria, was
charged with this enrolment in Judea. In
accordance with the imperial decree each
family had to repair to its own city to be
there inscribed in the public registers.
Though the Blessed Virgin and St. Joseph
were settled at Nazareth, in Galilee, their
family belonged not to that province. Being both descended from the royal house of
David, Bethlehem, a small town of the
tribe of Juda, was the cradle of their
family. It was, therefore, to Bethlehem
that they had both to repair. It was a
journey of nearly thirty leagues, therefore
both long and toilsome, especially to the
young virgin about to become a mother;
and all the more so on account of having
to be performed in the inclement season of
winter. Nevertheless, without a complaint

or murmur, as soon as they became informed of the order of the emperor both
Mary and Joseph hastened to obey it; for
they knew that it was from God that
princes reign, and that to disobey their
laws was to disobey the will of God. Oh!
how easy and sweet would obedience become to us if, like Mary and Joseph, we
ever looked upon the commands of our
superiors as the manifestation of the will
of God!

After much toil and fatigues, borne with
patience and resignation, the holy way-
farers arrive at Bethlehem. It was the
termination of their journey, but not so of
their distress and sufferings. The whole
town was full of strangers; all the inns
were full. In vain then they sought shelter;
none would admit them. Repulsed on every
side, rejected by all, they at last retired
to a poor stable open to all the winds of
heaven. There, at midnight, in the depth
of winter, without aid, and destitute of all
human comfort, Mary brought to the world
her divine Son Jesus. As she had conceived miraculously and without prejudice
to her virginity, she brought forth without
pain and without ceasing to be a virgin.

As soon as He was born, Mary wrapped
Him in some poor clothing which she had
with her, and then laid Him in a manger
on a poor bed of straw. Such was the
cradle of the Son of God made man, coming
into the world in order to save us; such
the palace wherein the King of heaven and
earth chose to be born.

What a lesson for us is the stable of
Bethlehem! We see there the three most
holy of persons, Jesus, Mary, and Joseph.
We behold them slighted, exposed to all
the inclemency of the season, reduced to
the utmost misery; their only shelter a
poor stable, their only bed a little damp
straw, and even these did not belong to
them: they had not whereon to lay their
head. But why was it that Jesus Christ
chose to be born in a state so lowly, so
poor, and surrounded by so much sufferings? It was to give us a pattern of
detachment, of penance and mortification;
it was to point out to us the way to heaven.
There are three ordinary sources from which
almost all our faults proceed—attachment
to creatures and the things of this world,
the love of pleasure and enjoyment, a repugnance to humiliations and sufferings

found him at the bottom of the river, and taking
him by the hair they brought him to land.   Every
one came to see the dead body; but they were
agreeably surprised to find the child full of life,
unhurt, and quite joyful.   They questioned him
how he had remained so long under water without
injury; he replied, that immediately after he fell
in he saw a beautiful lady who came to his aid,
and with her own hands prevented the water from
touching him, and that he had no doubt she was
the Blessed Virgin, Mother of God.   Roenata, full
of gratitude towards his heavenly protectress, never
ceased to honour and serve her during the remain-
der of his life, which he closed with the glory of
martyrdom (*Bollandists, July* 14*th*).

PRACTICE.

Let us go often in spirit to the stable of Bethlehem, and there beholding Jesus and Mary in
misery and suffering, let us learn to bear up under
all the miseries and sufferings of this life; let us
learn to sanctify our trials and make them meritorious for heaven, by uniting them to the sufferings and trials of Jesus Christ and His divine
Mother.

TENTH DAY.

THE SHEPHERDS AND THE MAGI COME TO BETH- LEHEM TO ADORE THE INFANT JESUS.

HARDLY had the Blessed Virgin given birth to the Divine Infant, when an angel all beaming with light appeared to some poor shepherds, who were keeping the night watch over their flocks, and announced to them that the Messiah, for whose coming they had so long sighed, was just born in a stable at Bethlehem. Obedient to the voice of the angel, who summoned them to the Saviour's crib, the shepherds hastened to set out for Bethlehem, where they found the child wrapped in swaddling clothes and laid in a manger. Full of a lively faith, they recognised Him as their God, prostrated themselves at His feet, adored Him with the profoundest respect, and devoted themselves for ever to His service; thus, having rendered Him their homage, they returned to their flocks, praising and giving thanks to the Lord. Thus it was, by their docility to grace and their lively faith, that these poor shepherds merited to become the first adorers and first disciples of Jesus.

ing that corrupting book, relinquish that
society, avoid that person whose conduct is
a cause of scandal to you.   Have we heark-
ened to these holy inspirations?   Have
we not slighted and resisted them?   Have
we not sometimes sought to stifle remorse
of conscience because it teased and impor-
tuned us?   And have not our resistance
and unfaithfulness to grace been the cause
of God's abandoning us to ourselves?   "I
have called on you and you would not hear
me," says our Lord; I have invited you
and you have rejected my invitation.   I
now withdraw my graces from you, and
deliver you up to the desires of your heart.
Let no such dreadful evil ever befall us,
O my God!   Strike, punish us, deprive us
of earthly goods, of health, of life itself, but
take not Thy grace from us; for such a
loss would be the greatest of misfortunes,
as it would be the cause of our eternal
ruin.   After the example of the shepherds
and the wise men, let us be faithful to grace,
let us never resist it, let us obey with
promptitude its salutary teachings, and this
divine grace, along with making us happy
and being our consolation on earth, will
secure us an eternal recompense in heaven.

EXAMPLE.

Docility to Grace.

A certain youth, on the occasion of making his first holy Communion, had made the following resolution:—"If I ever should have the misfortune to fall into mortal sin I will go to confession at once, and I will never lie down to rest without being first reconciled to God." Some months later he happened to commit a grievous sin. It was on a Saturday that this misfortune befel him, and as he lived at a distance from the church, he at first said to himself, " To-morrow when I go to Mass I will seek out my confessor and make my confession." But forthwith he remembered his promise, and he heard, besides, something that said to him, " Do what thou hast promised; go to confession." However, he still hesitated ; in this internal conflict he threw himself on his knees to implore the guidance of the Blessed Virgin, and for that intention recited a " Hail, Mary." Scarcely had he concluded his prayer than he felt himself strongly urged to go to confession at once. He arose and went in search of his confessor. On his return he met his mother, who asked where he had been. " I have been to confession," he said, with a countenance beaming with happiness and joy. "I had been guilty of sin, and I would not go to rest until I had forgiveness; but now that I have recovered the friendship of God I will rest in peace and sleep undisturbed." His mother used to let him remain in bed a little longer on Sundays than on other days. Accordingly she did not call him next

morning till seven o'clock. Knocking at his door
and calling him by his name she got no response.
A quarter of an hour later, as he still slept, his
mother returned, and, impatient at his not reply-
ing, she went into his chamber and approached his
bed. Strange! he did not stir, he did not breathe!
She took his hand, it was rigid and cold; she
looked into his face in affright, and uttering piercing cries she fell insensible to the ground. The
boy had died during the night. O happy youth
in having been obedient to grace, and not putting
off confession till the morrow! Let us imitate his
example, and never go to sleep with an unrepented
mortal sin on our conscience (*Le Mois de ma Mère.
R. P. Terwecoren*).

PRACTICE.

Let us never resist grace; it would be for us the
greatest of misfortunes. How many sinners have
been lost, how many souls have fallen into hell
through having stifled remorse of conscience and
refused to listen to that interior voice urging them
to repent and make their peace with God!

———

ELEVENTH DAY.

THE BLESSED VIRGIN PRESENTS HERSELF IN THE TEMPLE FOR HER PURIFICATION, AND TO MAKE THE OFFERING OF HER DIVINE SON.

THE law of Moses required that, forty
days after the birth of a male infant, the

mother should present herself in the Temple
to be purified, and to offer to God her new-
born son. It is evident that Mary was not
bound by that law; she was under no obligation to present herself to be purified, since
she never had ceased to be all virginal and
pure; it was not incumbent on her to bring
thither her Son to offer Him to the Lord,
for that Son was God, and as God He was
above all such laws. Still, to set us an
example of obedience, Mary conformed to
a law that did not bind; and accordingly,
when the forty days fixed for her purification were accomplished, she took in her
arms the Divine Infant and repaired to Jerusalem. Arrived in the Temple, she submitted, like the lowliest of her sex, to all
the ceremonies of purification; omitting
nothing, however painful or humiliating it
might be. Without in any way asserting
her wonderful privileges of being at once
virgin and mother of God, she fell in with
the crowd, she placed herself in the ranks
of the poor and sinful. The law prescribed
two sorts of offering—one for the poor and
the other for the rich; Mary made the
offering of the poor. The law commanded
ordinary mothers, who had contracted this

legal stain, to offer a victim of expiation.
Mary, as if one of them, made this offering;
in a word, she submitted to purification as
if she had been sullied, as if she had for-
feited her virginity. Why, O Mary, this
ceremony of purification? did you not
know how the angel from heaven assured
you that you were the purest of virgins,
the holiest of creatures? Mary was not
ignorant of this; but the higher she was
raised in the sight of God, the more she
abased herself in the sight of men, to con-
found our pride; the more reasons she had
for considering herself exempt from the
law, the more exactly did she fulfil it, to
condemn our acts of rebellion and disobe-
dience.

According to the law, Mary was also to offer
her Divine Son in the Temple. She therefore took her Jesus in her arms and brought
Him before the altar, there she presents
Him to the Eternal Father as the sole Victim
capable of appeasing His wrath, resigns
Him unreservedly to all the requirements
of His dread justice, and unhesitatingly
offers Him as the Victim who by His death
was to purchase our salvation. What a
sacrifice was this for the heart of a mother!

But that which most of all tended to crush the tender heart of Mary was the sad prediction of the prophet Simeon; he foretold that this Infant which he took into his arms should one day be persecuted, insulted, outraged, and put to death, and that a sword of sorrow should also pierce her heart. This prediction was as the point of the sword to Mary, which thenceforth continued to lacerate her heart, and which it succeeded in completely piercing on Calvary at the foot of the cross. It was, then—this day of her purification and presentation of her Son in the Temple—a day of great sorrow to the Blessed Virgin; but it was one, at the same time, of great merit by her exactitude and zeal in the perfect observance of the law.

Alas! how far are we from being exact like Mary in fulfilling the laws of God! Mary submits to a law that no way bound her, and we are unwilling to comply with those that are of strictest obligation to us. God enjoins on us to keep His commandments, and we daily violate them, and frequently, even many times in the day. He threatens us with the severest penalties and most rigorous chastisements if we commit

sin, and we seem to say : "I know that
sin is offensive to Thee, that it displeases
and outrages Thee : no matter, I will commit it, and that in Thy presence and under
Thy eyes. I know that Thou canst punish
me and cast me into hell : no matter, I will
gratify my passions and give up to the
wicked desires of my heart." If our fel-
low-man held us suspended over an abyss,
would we have the temerity to insult and
outrage him whilst he thus held our life in
his hands? Our life is in the hands of God ;
He holds us suspended over the abyss of
hell, over the fiery gulf; at any moment
He could cast us into it, and we dare to
offer Him insult and outrage ! we dare to
provoke His wrath and His vengeance !
What blindness ! what madness ! Let us
now form the firm and sincere resolution
never again to offend God, but to faithfully
observe all His commandments, and we
shall thus secure in this life the joy and
peace which proceed from a good conscience,
and perfect and unending happiness in the
life hereafter.

EXAMPLE.

Mary deplores the Violation of the Law of God.

On Saturday, the 19th September, 1846, being
the vigil of the Feast of Our Lady of Dolours,
Melanie Mathieu, aged 14, and Maximin Giraud,
aged 11, both of the commune of La Salette, in
the diocese of Grenoble, happened to conduct the
flocks of which they were in charge to a level plain
in the mountains, distant two leagues from any
habitation. About midday, having eaten their
frugal repast, they went to put their wallets beside
a spring which at the time had become dried up;
after which, contrary to their custom, they both
went to sleep. They soon awoke, and, uneasy at
not seeing their cattle, they hastened away in
search of them. Ascending an eminence they discovered them lying over against them at a little
distance. They then descended to take away the
wallets which they had left beside the dry bed of
the stream. All at once a light more brilliant
than the sun appeared to them, in the midst of
which they saw a lady seated on a stone. Her
attitude was that of one who was a prey to the
most intense grief; her face was bathed in tears,
but her tears fell not to the earth, they vanished
like sparks of fire. On her brow there was a crown
of roses and a brilliant diadem. A white kerchief
garlanded also with roses, was on her bosom. At
this sight the two children were seized with terror,
but the lady arose, crossed her arms, and in a
sweet, kind voice said: "Fear not, my children,
I am come to make a great announcement to you."

Reassured by her words of kindness the two little
shepherds approached. The Queen of Heaven also
advanced towards them, and, shedding tears, said
that she had long mourned that she could no
longer stay the hand of her Divine Son, whose
anger was aroused against mankind on account of
their crimes, particularly on account of blasphemy
of the sacred name of God and the desecration of
the Lord's Day ; that it was on this account that
the fruits of the earth had begun to fail, and that
if those crimes were continued the punishment of
them would also become greater. Having made
these sad announcements and commanded them to
communicate them to all the people, she confided
to each a secret which they have never been willing
to divulge. She then ascended from the earth and
disappeared, leaving the little shepherds amazed
with what had just taken place. To perpetuate
the memory of this miraculous apparition the
Bishop of Grenoble has had a noble church erected
on the mountain of La Salette ; the Sovereign
Pontiff has enriched it with precious indulgences,
and the faithful constantly crowd thither from all
parts to implore the help and protection of the
Mother of God *(Extract from the "Notice sur
Notre-Dame de la Salette")*.

PRACTICE.

Let us faithfully observe all the commandments
of God.   Let us not forget that it is our violations
of God's holy law that draw upon us His anger
and His chastisements.   Let us ask pardon for our
offences, and promise that we will be faithful to
Him for the time to come.

TWELFTH DAY.

THE BLESSED VIRGIN, TO SAVE THE DIVINE INFANT, FLIES INTO EGYPT.

MARY had learned from the mouth of the aged Simeon that her Son should be exposed to persecution from the wicked. This prediction was soon verified. Hardly had she returned home after her purification in the Temple when an angel appeared in sleep to St. Joseph, and said to him: " Arise, take the Child and his Mother and fly into Egypt, and be there until I shall tell thee. For it will come to pass that Herod will seek the Child to destroy Him" (Matt. ii.). Joseph at once arose, and, taking Jesus and His holy Mother with him, forthwith set out for Egypt. Herod expected that the wise men would return to Jerusalem to give him an account of their journey as he had told them. He awaited them some days, but having ascertained that they had gone back to their own country by another way, he gave vent to his rage, and formed the horrible design of murdering all the male children that were in Bethlehem and in all

the borders thereof from two years old and
under. He believed Jesus to be still at Bethlehem, and hoped to include Him in this
cruel slaughter. He accordingly sent soldiers with orders to execute at once this san-
guinary project. The wretch was only too
literally obeyed by his infamous satellites!
These poor innocents were quickly de-
spatched without exception or pity; blood
flowed in every house. On every side were
heard the voice of lamentation and cries
of despair: the unhappy mothers bewailed
their children, torn from their arms, but-
chered before their very eyes, and were not
to be consoled. Good reason, indeed, they
had to weep! But whilst they mourned
for their children on earth, their children
were rejoicing with God in heaven; having
shed their blood for Jesus Christ, they are
numbered amongst the saints and martyrs.

The fate of Mary was little better than
that of the poor mothers of Bethlehem.
Constrained to fly precipitately, and in the
middle of the night, she had to leave her
country, her relatives, her friends, to go
into a strange and idolatrous land, where
she knew no one and had no means of sub-
sistence. She had to traverse more than

a hundred leagues, and that at an inclement season and with the sacred Infant in
her arms; to travel over a vast and frightful desert where she found neither shelter,
nor help, nor provisions. Ah, who can tell
all that Mary had to suffer during this long
and painful journey! Habituated, however, from infancy to adore the designs of
God in all things, she cheerfully submitted
to His holy will, and resigned herself with
confidence to the direction of His divine
Providence.

The Providence of God watches over us,
governs and directs us. Nothing happens
to us unless by His order or permission; a
single hair does not fall from our head
without the permission of our heavenly
Father. Oh! what a consolation to think
that we have a tender Father on high who
constantly cares for us, who wills nothing
but what is for our welfare and happiness!
Let us, therefore, put all our trust in Him,
and whatever be the trials or afflictions
through which we have to pass, let us
adore and bless this divine Providence.
But particularly with regard to the salvation of our soul should we repose our confidence in God. Why, in truth, should we

not have the utmost confidence in a God
who has so much loved us, who has done
so much for us, who has shed the last drop
of His blood for our salvation?   However
great may be our sins we should not despair of His mercy, for it is infinitely
greater than even our malice and ingrati-
tude.   But neither let us abuse His goodness by sinning by reason of it the more
freely; let us not say: "Later on I will
break off this bad habit, I will withdraw
from this sinful occasion; but there is time
enough; God is good and will pardon me
when I turn to Him."   How many sinners
are lost, plunged into hell through this mis-
called confidence!   God is always ready to
pardon us when we sincerely have recourse
to Him, but He often denies time for repentance to those who wilfully continue in
sin.   He has promised pardon to the peni-
tent, and not to-morrow to the sinner.

EXAMPLE.

Confidence in God.

A young Italian soldier, aged twenty-two, who
served in the French army, was sentenced to death
for having wounded a comrade and raised a weapon

against one of his officers. On the 15th October,
1858, the day before that fixed for his execution,
he was told that he had only some hours to live.
At this intelligence he gave himself up to the most
violent despair. In vain did the chaplain try to
calm him and to awaken his confidence in God by
recalling to his mind the goodness and mercy of
our Lord. He replied to all his exhortations only
with impiety and blasphemy, and though he allowed him to come to him again, the chaplain found
him in no better dispositions than before. The
minister of God, seeing how unavailing were his
efforts, had another priest brought. Both together
hastened to the side of the unhappy criminal, but
all their prayers and exhortations continued without effect. Without, however, losing hope, the
priest began to speak to him of the Blessed Virgin;
told him how she is the consoler of the afflicted, the
refuge of sinners; and urged him to put his trust
in her. At the name of Mary, the countenance of
the prisoner brightened, and a change seemed to
take place in his heart. The priest presented him
with a medal of the Blessed Virgin, representing
our Lady of Victories. The prisoner took it
thankfully, and after looking on it attentively an
instant: "Who is the Infant," he said, "that the
Blessed Virgin holds in her arms?" "It is her
Son Jesus, our Saviour." "Why has He his arms
stretched out?" "It is to receive all sinners, and
press them to His heart; see how He stretches out
His arms to you, He invites you to come to Him;
resign yourself to His love." At the sight of our
Saviour opening His arms for all sinners, hope was
reawakened in the breast of the prisoner; grace

triumphed, and he cried out: "Give me Italian
books that I may prepare myself for the Sacraments." It was then midnight. He spent three
hours examining his conscience and preparing himself for confession with many groans and tears.
At three o'clock he made his confession, and after
that appeared as if quite a new man. Perfectly
resigned to his fate, he now only thought of the
happiness of receiving his God. At five, his confessor said Mass in his cell, and administered to
him the Holy Communion; and a second Mass of
thanksgiving was then celebrated. During the
whole time, the condemned man seemed absorbed
in the most profound fervour and piety. The
moment of departure at last came. After being
invested with the scapular, and putting around
his neck a little cross, he arose, took a large crucifix
in his hands, on which he kept his eyes constantly
fixed, and advanced towards the place of execution,
repeating every instant: "Holy Mary, Mother of
God, pray for me! Most merciful Jesus, who died
for me on the cross, have mercy on me in this
dreadful moment!" Having arrived at the place
of execution, he begged a last absolution from the
priest, which he received with the deepest humility,
embraced his confessor, and having several times
repeated: "My God, Thy will be done!" he let
them bandage his eyes, and placed himself on his
knees. Almost at the same moment, a discharge
of musketry was heard, and the poor fellow was
dead. His body fell bathed in blood; but his soul,
full of confidence in God, entered into eternity,
there, we hope, to chant for ever the mercies of
Jesus and His Divine Mother (*Le Pouvoir de Marie*

PRACTICE.

We should never despair of our salvation; but we should also never cease to labour for it; for, notwithstanding that God desires that we should be saved, yet He will not save us if we, on our part, do not what depends on us. "God who has created you without yourself," says St. Augustine, "will not save you without yourself."

THIRTEENTH DAY.

THE BLESSED VIRGIN LEAVES EGYPT AND RE-TURNS TO NAZARETH.

THE happy moment at length is come when the Blessed Virgin and St. Joseph could leave Egypt to return to their native land. Herod, their persecutor, died, and went before God to account for his guilty conduct. Hardly had that cruel prince compassed the massacre of the children at Bethlehem, when the hand of God smote him in a most signal and terrible manner; he was at the height of his wicked career when he was seized with a dreadful malady; a consuming fire took possession of his frame, and raged even in the marrow of his bones.

From the effects of this disease his flesh putrified and fell off in shreds. Myriads of worms became engendered in his wounds, devoured him alive, and caused him the most horrible sufferings. His whole body was as a putrid corpse; his punishment was insupportable; it was but the just chastisement of his sins, and the retaliation for all the innocent blood shed by this impious and barbarous prince. Happy, even then, if he had profited by his sufferings to become converted, and to make his peace with God! But, like the greater number of those who have grown old in iniquity, instead of repenting, he only became the more hardened in his crimes, and he died as he had lived, impenitent.

As soon as Herod had breathed his last, an angel appeared again to St. Joseph in sleep, and said to him: "Arise, and take the Child and His Mother, and go into the land of Israel. For they are dead who sought the life of the Child." Ever docile and obedient, Joseph arose promptly, took Jesus and His divine Mother, and set out for the land of his fathers. After the endurance of much sufferings and fatigues, the Blessed Virgin and St. Joseph arrived in

Palestine. What was their grief and alarm, when they learned that Archelaus, the son of Herod, had succeeded his father in the government of Judea! Fearing that the new king in inheriting the throne of his father had also inherited his feelings of hatred against Jesus, they durst not advance, and knew not what to do; whilst they were in this state of perplexity, they received during night a warning from heaven, that they were to retire to Galilee. They accordingly set out for that province, and settled at Nazareth, where, as before, they led a life of prayer, poverty, and labour.

How admirable was the submission of the Blessed Virgin and St. Joseph to the appointments of Divine Providence! An angel commands them to go into Egypt, and they went; he orders them to return into Judea, and they do so; he directs them to retire into Galilee, and they repair thither. Never the least murmur, or the slightest impatience, no matter what amount of trouble or difficulty they encountered. They knew the will of God; that was all sufficient for them; they at once obeyed it, were wholly submissive to it, and fulfilled it with eager-

ness. Is it thus that we conform ourselves
to the will of God in the various sacrifices
it demands of us in all the events of life?
Let us ever bear in mind, that nothing
occurs on earth without the permission of
God. Sickness, infirmities, accidents, loss
of goods, death of parents and friends, the
persecutions, even, that we meet with from
our fellow man, all, all are in accordance
with the designs of God. He has foreseen
them, He orders or permits them for our
sanctification and salvation.

Let us adore the designs of God in our
regard; and whether He raises us up or
humbles us; whether He consoles us or sends
us afflictions; whether He bestows worldly
goods upon us or reduces us to indigence;
whether he gives us health or sends us
sickness; in whatever manner He disposes
of us, let us always be submissive to His
holy will.

"The Lord gave, and the Lord hath
taken away," said holy Job; "as it pleased
the Lord, so is it done; blessed be the
name of the Lord" (Job i. 21). Let us be
ever thus conformable to the will of God,
and we shall act as true Christians, for the

whole Christian life consists in willing that
which God wills, and wishing for nothing
save only as He wills.

EXAMPLE.

Submission to the will of God.

In a certain town, in the diocese of Arras, there
lived a person well known for her edifying life and
many good works. This person was attacked by a
malady that, for more than six months baffled all
the skill of the physicians, and was the source of
great affliction to her family. Her sufferings were
intense, and her weakness extreme. Her limbs,
which were withered and almost completely power-
less, prevented her from changing her position;
she was so enfeebled, that every one expected her
immediate death. In the early part of January,
1854, some of her friends, alarmed at her condition,
proposed to make a novena to the Blessed Virgin
in her behalf. "I consent," she replied, "on the
condition that you ask for me not my cure, but for
the perfect accomplishment of the will of God; for
whether He is pleased to restore me to health, or to
prove me by sickness, I submit myself entirely to His
holy will." Her pious friends met together before
the altar of Mary each day of the novena, earnestly
imploring the Mother of God to intercede for her
who was so dear to them. The invalid united her
own prayers to theirs. Still her state continued
unchanged. During the night preceding the last

day of the novena, her sufferings even became so
excruciating, that, for the first time, involuntary
cries of pain escaped her. Those about her thought
that her end was at hand. Next day at half-past six,
she received Holy Communion; at seven, the holy
sacrifice of the Mass was offered for her; towards
half-past seven, she requested the person who attended her to bring her clothes. She refused doing
so at first, thinking it to be only a whim of the
sick person. Finally, she complied with the re-
quest; what was her astonishment when she saw
her at once make use of her limbs, dress herself, and
get out of bed with a readiness that indicated a
complete freedom from all suffering! The first
thought of the invalid, thus suddenly restored to
health, was to cast herself in thanksgiving before
her heavenly benefactress. She proceeded forthwith
to the church without assistance, accompanied by
her relatives, who could hardly believe their eyes,
so much were they astonished. Having heard the
holy Mass, she returned home with equal facility,
and without experiencing any fatigue. This incontestable fact, regarded as supernatural, even by
the physicians, awakened in the hearts of many,
sentiments of filial confidence towards the Mother
of God. May it produce the like sentiments in us,
and lead us to venerate the august Queen of
Heaven! (*L'Univers*, *February 12th*, 1854).

PRACTICE.

In adversity as in prosperity, in sorrows as in
joy, in sickness as in health, in all the events of
life, let us submit ourselves entirely and unre-

servedly to the will of God. Let our words be ever: God wills it, God permits it, and He wills or permits nothing save for my greater good; His holy will be done! blessed be His holy name!

FOURTEENTH DAY.

THE BLESSED VIRGIN LOSES HER DIVINE SON, AND FINDS HIM IN THE TEMPLE.

THE Blessed Virgin and St. Joseph went regularly every year to Jerusalem for the celebration of the Paschal Feast. When Jesus was twelve years old, they went up to Jerusalem according to custom and brought Him with them. Arrived at the Temple, the holy travellers acquitted themselves with exactitude of all that the law prescribed. They passed in retirement and prayer the days consecrated to the celebration of the Passover; and these ended, Mary and Joseph, in company with their relatives and friends set out on their return to Nazareth. When leaving, not perceiving the Divine Child, they concluded that He was in company with persons of their acquaintance, and had no apprehension on His

account. Thus they journeyed a whole
day, hoping each moment that Jesus would
rejoin them. Now, however, as the day
closed, and He did not appear, they felt
the greatest uneasiness on His account.
They sought Him amongst their relatives
and friends, but in vain; no person had
seen Him, no one had any intelligence
regarding Him. What was then their
grief, their trouble! They at once turned
back in search of Him, they returned to
Jerusalem; but their first efforts to obtain
information about Him were unsuccessful.
It was not until after three days' anxious
and toilsome search that they found Him
in the Temple, seated amidst the doctors of
the law, interrogating them and answering
their questions, astonishing everyone by
the wisdom and knowledge He displayed.
Mary and Joseph joined the crowd that
pressed around to hear Jesus; they heard
His praises echoed on all sides, and were
filled with admiration. As the loss of Him
had caused them deep pain and sorrow, so
His presence gave them the greatest happiness and joy. How happy it is to find
Jesus again after having lost Him! What
sweet consolation His divine presence dif-

fuses in souls that are afflicted! The grief
that Mary had experienced in the absence
of her Divine Son was so great and deep,
that she could not help uttering her loving
complaint. "Son," she said, "why hast
Thou done so to us? behold, Thy father
and I have sought Thee sorrowing!" "How
is it that you sought Me?" He said to them;
"did you not know that I must be about
My Father's business?"

We are to remember that, if the Blessed
Virgin and St. Joseph had the misfortune
to lose Jesus, it was only through inadver-
tence, and altogether without their being in
the slightest way to blame. Alas! how
often do we lose Him wilfully, through our
own fault, by sin? Yes, by sin we lose
God, we lose our soul, we lose everything.
By sin we revolt against God, we expel
Him from our heart, we become His perse-
cutors, His executioners; we crucify Him
again, according to the expression of St.
Paul. What a crime! to crucify our
Creator, our Saviour, our God? By sin we
lose our own soul, we yield it up to the
demon; Satan possesses himself of it, dis-
honours and degrades it, drags it through
the mire of vice and evil passions, and

tramples it under foot as a vile slave.
What a degradation and abasement is this!
By sin we lose heaven. One single mortal
sin, one only sinful thought wilfully consented to, would be enough to deprive us
of heaven, and precipitate us into hell. See
the angels : they were the noblest creatures
of God; they were His messengers, His
favourites. Yet, a great number of them
had the misfortune to commit a sin, one
sole sin of thought, the sin of a moment,
committed only once ; and on the instant,
without giving them time for repentance,
they were hurled, without pity and for
eternity, into the abyss of hell! Let us
then dread sin, since God has punished it
so rigorously even in His angels. Let us
never again yield deliberately to it; but if
unhappily we should commit it, let us not
remain in that sad state; let us lose no
time in arising out of it lest we should be
surprised by death. How many are now
numbered amongst the reprobate for having
deferred their repentance! They said:
to-morrow I will put my soul in order ; and
a sudden death, an unforeseen accident,
took them at once out of life and plunged
them for ever into hell. Let us follow the

counsel of the Holy Ghost : delay not to be converted to the Lord, and defer it not from day to day, lest His wrath should come of a sudden, and in the time of His vengeance He should destroy thee.

EXAMPLE.

Fear of Sin.

On the slope of a hill that skirts the road from Insprock to Milan, a young girl, named Mary, watched her flock, and chanted a sweet hymn to the Blessed Virgin, her patroness. A director of the chief theatre of Milan, who chanced to pass at the moment, no sooner heard the voice of the young shepherdess, than, stopping his carriage, he drew near the better to hear her. He was enchanted with her melodious voice ; never before had he listened to one so sweet, so rich, and of such extensive compass. "What a splendid voice!" he said "How well it would suit the theatre! What an acquisition it would prove!" Thus thinking, he approached the young girl. "Will you bring me to your mother?" he said. "But what will become of my flock? she replied. "Do not mind about your flock," he said. "I will give you a hundred, a thousand times their value." "Why do you wish to see my mother?" she asked. "To make her happy in taking her out of poverty," he answered; "I wish you to come with me; I will make you the leading singer of Milan, and your fortune is made." "I want not your fortune," she said, "I could not save my soul in your theatre. I have often heard it said, that one should lose her own soul who makes herself the occasion of sin to others. Therefore do not reckon on me." The director seeing he made no way with the young girl, sought out her mother, who, delighted to discover a means of emerging from poverty, urged her daughter to agree to the proposed arrangement; but neither the pressing solicitations of her mother, nor the dazzling prospects held out by the director could shake her resolution, and she firmly refused. He gave her till the next day to reconsider her decision. What a sad night it was to the poor child! On the one hand, she thought of her aged mother, and she would gladly have taken her out of poverty; on the other hand, she said to herself: "If I accept this offer I trample my baptismal vows under foot, and shall lose my soul." She passed the whole night in prayer; addressing herself now to God, now to the Blessed Virgin, or to her guardian angel, and each time she heard within her conscience something that kept saying to her: "Do not consent; you would be leaving Jesus to go over to Satan." The morning come, the mother returned to the charge. "Have you decided to accept the offers that have been made you?" she said. "No, mother," she replied, "it is impossible." "You shall do it," she said, in wrath; "I insist upon it; I command you." "Mother," she replied, "order me to do anything else, and I will obey you with delight; but I must not offend God, I cannot forfeit my eternal happiness." "Retire," said the mother, in great anger; "go prepare yourself; we set out in an hour's time." The young girl went away to consider what she should do; suddenly a thought struck her, and she formed an heroic resolution. Having heard it said that the loss of the front teeth makes a complete change in the voice, and deprives it of a great deal of its strength and sweetness, she approached a window and deliberately broke two of her teeth against a projecting stone, after which she returned joyfully to her mother. The mother thought that she had changed her resolution; but the director, already perceiving the change in her voice, and knowing well the cause, was filled with admiration of her heroic courage; he renounced his project, and exhorted the mother not to persecute a daughter so deserving of her esteem and affection. See what a generous sacrifice this girl made in order to avoid sin. How should her example make us blush, we who show so little courage in resisting temptation! (*La Devotion à Marie en Examples*).

PRACTICE.

The only real evil for us to fear is sin. Sin will deprive us for ever of the sight of God, and keep us out of heaven; sin, one mortal sin, will deliver us over to remorse, to despair, to the never-ending fire of hell. Let us, therefore, fly sin as we would the face of a serpent.

FIFTEENTH DAY.

LIFE OF THE HOLY FAMILY AT NAZARETH.

A BEAUTIFUL spectacle was that presented by the Holy Family at Nazareth. Every virtue reigned there—piety, peace, union, and love of labour. We must not think that the Blessed Virgin and St. Joseph lived in indolence and idleness; on the contrary, they led a hard and laborious life; humble labourers, simple artizans, they toiled, and gained their daily bread in the sweat of their brow. They knew that all are condemned to labour in punishment of sin, and they conformed themselves to this degree with joy and in a spirit of penance. They fulfilled the irksome duties of their state of life with exactitude and fidelity, and without a murmur or complaint; they offered and referred to God their trials, their labours, and all their actions; they sanctified them by prayer; whilst their hands were employed in work, their souls were fixed on God, and engaged in prayer. They bore with patience and resignation the crosses and afflictions which the Lord sent them; they blessed and adored His divine provi-

dence in all things. Thus, sanctifying the
common, ordinary actions of life, the Blessed
Virgin and St. Joseph attained to that high
degree of sanctity and perfection, that
merited for them so high a place in heaven.
But, not only by the example of the
Blessed Virgin and St. Joseph are we taught
that we can sanctify ourselves in fulfilling
the common, ordinary duties of life, we are,
moreover, taught the same lesson by the
example of Jesus Christ Himself. He was
God, He was all powerful; in coming on
earth He could have made choice of high
and distinguished position, and He chose,
instead, a condition the most humble and
obscure; He could have wrought miracles,
and elicited the admiration of the world by
the splendour of His deeds and His virtues,
and He shut Himself up in the workshop
of a poor artizan; He devoted Himself to
the performance of the simplest and most
commonplace occupations; He had a right
to the obedience of all creatures, and He
obeyed the Blessed Virgin and St. Joseph.
Behold the example set us by Jesus Christ
to teach us that in leading a life of poverty,
obscurity, toil, and labour, the more conformable is our life to His, and the more

easily, therefore, can we secure our salvation;
to teach us, moreover, that true sanctity
does not consist in the performance of
extraordinary actions, but in the faithful
accomplishment of the duties of our state
of life, however humble or unimportant
they may be.

We can all become great saints by doing
nothing beyond what we do each day.
Most of the saints did no more than what
we ourselves are doing. There was no
difference between their actions and ours
but the motive and intention. That which
we do from mere habit, and from human,
earthly motives, they performed through
motives of faith and religion; that which
we do from necessity, and frequently with
repugnance, they performed with joy and as
a duty. They referred everything to God,
they did all for His glory, according to the
precept of St. Paul. How many Christians
who have toiled and suffered much during
their lives shall, nevertheless, appear before
God with their hands empty from not
having taken care to offer and refer to Him
their sufferings and their actions! Let us
then refer everything to God, and do it
solely for His glory. Let us say to Him at

the commencement of each day: My God
I offer and consecrate to Thee my labours,
my trials, and sufferings; I accept them in
penance for my sins; I unite them to the
trials, suffering, and labours which Thou
hast borne for love of me. From time to
time during the day renew this offering of
your actions to God; thus doing all our
works, even those that are the least important will become great and precious in the
eyes of God; they will acquire a supernatural merit, and will form one day our
glory and our happiness in heaven.

EXAMPLE.

A Christian Family.

It was the year 1812; a general conscription
took place, obliging all to join the army who were
capable of bearing arms. Amongst the new conscripts
were the two sons of a virtuous Christian family.
Having each received a medal of the Blessed Virgin, the two young soldiers tenderly embraced their
afflicted parents, and set out to join their regiment.
The French army, which advanced into the heart
of Russia was at first successful; but it was soon
destroyed and decimated by the inclemency of the
climate, and was forced to fall back and beat a retreat. Having reached the banks of the Beresina,
men and horses cast themselves in utter disorder

on the bridges that were hastily constructed, and
the shore and bed of the river were strewn with the
dead and dying; in the precipitancy of flight, even
the wounded were abandoned. Amongst these
latter was one of the brothers of whom we speak.
A bullet had fractured his shoulder, and left him
expiring amidst a heap of slain. In this extremity,
he recommended himself to the Blessed Virgin; he
took her medal into his hand, pressed it to his
heart, and cried with an expiring voice: "Mary!
refuge of the unfortunate, have pity on me, come
to my help." His prayer was not long unheard.
Presently a detachment of the Russian army
passed along the bank of the river, and a young
officer remarking something that shone on the
breast of one of the soldiers lying on the field of
battle, approached, and discovered that it was a
medal of the Blessed Virgin which the dying man
had let fall from his failing grasp; the officer took
it up with eagerness, placed it in his bosom, and
perceiving that the wounded man still breathed,
had him carried to a neighbouring house in order
to look to his wounds. Whilst this poor wounded
man was thus rescued on the field of battle, his
brother, who was ignorant of his fate, was taken
prisoner, and was sent away to the interior of
Siberia to labour in the mines. There a hard and
brutal master daily loaded him with work, and
gave him hardly any food. Thus he wasted
away from hard treatment and grief. His sole
consolation was his medal. Often, when alone, he
pressed it to his lips, bathing it with his tears, and
exclaiming: "Oh Mary! comforter of the afflicted,
help me, deliver me." Mary was not insensible

to his petitions. His master had a son, a young
officer, who had been engaged in the late campaign.
Friendly relations soon sprung up between the
young Russian officer and the young Frenchman;
they saw each other every day. One evening as
they were together in the officer's apartment, suddenly the eyes of the prisoner became fixed on a
certain object; it was a medal of the Blessed
Virgin; he approached, gazed upon it, and exclaiming: "Oh, my poor brother!" he fell to the
ground in a swoon. The officer hastened to raise
him, and as soon as he had recovered consciousness,
asked him the cause of his grief. "I had a brother
in the army with me," he said; "but, alas! I see
plainly that he was slain on the field of battle, for
that is his medal." "Take comfort," replied the
officer, "your brother is not dead, it was I who
saved his life." He then related what has been
told already. "It was by my means that the
Blessed Virgin was pleased to save your brother,
and through me it is that she will save you also;
to-morrow you shall be free." The next day at
the earliest dawn, the two young friends, mounted
on two powerful chargers, set out in the direction
of France, and when they were sufficiently distant
no longer to apprehend pursuit, the officer stopped,
indicated to him the locality in which he should
find his brother, and saying: "Adieu, my friend!"
"Adieu, my liberator," the prisoner replied, and
embracing each other tenderly, they parted in tears.

Shortly after, on the 10th of August, 1813,
the two brothers re-entered their home, after being
absent from it ten months. It is impossible to
give an idea of the joy of this pious family in find-

yet come. Still, to show us that He could
refuse nothing to His holy mother, Jesus
caused water to be brought, and by an exercise of His omnipotence He changed it
miraculously into wine. This changing of
water into wine wrought at the marriage
of Cana, in Galilee, was the first public
miracle of our Saviour, and it was Mary
who obtained it by the efficacy of her intercession.

How great is the power of prayer offered
to God with confidence and faith! Behold
Mary: she prays Jesus to perform a miracle, and Jesus seems to refuse, saying
that His time for working miracles was not
yet come. Despite this seeming repulse
Mary is not discouraged; and Jesus, to reward her confidence and faith, works the
miracle which she asks. How efficacious
would be our prayers were they offered
with the like faith and confidence as that
of Mary! But, alas! how far removed
are we from such dispositions! When God
defers for a time to grant us what we ask,
we give ourselves up to diffidence and despondency; we give over praying, and we
hus deprive ourselves of those graces which
we would have obtained had we but per-

severed in prayer; for very often it is at
the moment when we think all hope is over
that we are nearest to be heard. If sometimes we obtain not what we ask, it is
because we pray badly, and then it is our
own fault; or because we ask for what
would be prejudicial to our salvation, and
then God hears us, not indeed by granting
us that which we ask, but other more precious graces. Thus, we ask to be freed
from a certain affliction, trouble, or malady,
and God, to prove us, allows it to continue; but by reason of our prayers He
grants us strength and courage to bear it
with patience; and instead of a temporal
grace that we petitioned for, and which
would have availed but for this life, God
grants us a spiritual grace that will bear
precious fruits for all eternity. Are we
not, then, heard, and even beyond our desires? Let us, then, pray with confidence,
let us pray with a strong faith, let us pray
above all with perseverance, and undoubtedly we shall obtain every grace of which
we stand in need; for God is a kind Father,
and ever hearkens to His children when
they pray with due dispositions.

EXAMPLE.

Efficacy of Prayer.

Some years since a celebrated preacher, Père Carboy, whilst preaching at Lyons, observed in one of his instructions that prayer offered with a lively faith, especially with a pure and innocent heart, could work a miracle. A young girl of nine or ten years of age who was present at once formed the resolution to ask for the conversion of her father and mother. Next day she sought the missionary, and said to him with tears and a voice broken by sobs—"Father, you said on yesterday that prayer offered with lively faith should obtain a miracle. Ever since I heard you say so I have not ceased to ask for the conversion of my father and mother; I have prayed, I have wept all night, and still my father and mother are not converted." "True, my child," replied the missionary, "I stated that prayer offered with a lively faith should obtain a miracle, but I did not say that the miracle would take place all at once; continue to pray and the miracle will be obtained." As the child had not made her first Communion, the missionary undertook to prepare her for it. Each day she returned, and each time she said: "Father, the miracle has not yet taken place; I pray, I weep before God, I ask of the Blessed Virgin the conversion of my parents, and yet they do not come to hear you. When, think you, will the miracle come to pass?" "Continue to pray," said the priest, "and the miracle will take place." On the day previous to that on which she was to make her first Communion with some other children, she came according to custom, received absolution with the piety of an angel, and as she returned home with a heart full of joy, thinking of the solemn act that was to take place on the morrow, she met a young cousin who embraced her with emotion, saying, "Bertha, do you not know? Oh! how happy I am! To-morrow, my father and mother are to receive Holy Communion with me." Then the poor child became sad, and her eyes filled with tears. She returned home where her parents impatiently expected her; but, instead of seeing her contented and happy, they saw her come back blinded with tears. "How is this, my child?" they asked; "you said how happy you should be on the eve of your first Communion, and see how sad you are." "I was happy but a moment ago, when I came from confession," replied the child; "but I met my cousin, who embraced me, saying that her father and mother were to approach Holy Communion with her on to-morrow. Then I said to myself: And I shall be alone: I shall not have the joy of seeing my father and mother beside me." "Yes, to-morrow you shall be alone," they answered, with tears in their eyes; "but in a few days you shall renew your first Communion, and we will accompany you to the Holy Table. We shall at once wait upon the priest who has prepared you for first Communion." Next day the victorious child conducted her father and mother to her confessor, saying to him: "Father you were right; the miracle is accomplished." Some days after, she saw them beside her at the Holy Table; she was overwhelmed with joy, all her desires were fulfilled.

Behold here the efficacy of prayer arising from a rightly disposed heart (*Le Messager de la Charité, 21st May,* 1859).

PRACTICE.

It is an undoubted truth that God always hears our prayers when they are performed aright. Let us then pray with faith, with confidence, with attention; let us pray particularly with great perseverance, and we most certainly shall be heard.

SEVENTEENTH DAY.

THE BLESSED VIRGIN ACCOMPANIES HER DIVINE SON IN HIS MISSIONARY JOURNEYS.

JESUS passed the three last years of His life amidst the severest labours, and sufferings without number. Our divine Saviour went continually from village to village, from province to province, to announce His Gospel, dispensing on all sides His graces and favours. He instructed the ignorant, converted sinners, consoled the afflicted, healed the sick, and raised the dead to life; but the more He did good and comforted the unfortunate, the more did the Scribes and Pharisees pursue Him with

their hatred and persecution. They in-
vented against Him the blackest calumnies,
they laid a thousand snares for Him, sought
to surprise Him, to seize upon His person
in order to put Him to death. Several
times He had to take to flight to escape
their criminal designs. O adorable Saviour,
what have you not borne to redeem us, to
snatch us from the fire of hell and purchase
the joys of heaven for us!

Whilst Jesus thus devoted Himself to
the painful labours of His public mission,
what happened to His most holy mother?
She shared the toils and sufferings of her
divine Son; she accompanied Him in His
evangelical wanderings throughout Judea
Who can say all that this tender mother
had to suffer during the three years of the
public life of Jesus? She beheld her beloved Son in the most absolute privation
and want; she saw Him overwhelmed with
fatigue and labours, and sorely tried by
troubles and opposition; she heard the calumnies that were charged against Him;
she was aware of the plots of which it was
sought to make Him the victim, the continual dangers to which He was exposed;
she knew that the Jews had resolved on

His death, and that they only awaited a
favourable moment in order to put their
wicked design into execution. What a
source of affliction was this to Mary, the
most tender and sensitive of mothers! Still
she resigned herself to it all, because she
knew that it was all directed to our salvation. O sacred mother, Mary, what sufferings have you not endured, what sacrifices
have you not made through love of us!
Suffer us not to be so unhappy as to forfeit
and make useless all that your divine Son
and you have suffered that we might be
saved.

Jesus and Mary have undergone everything for our salvation, and we do almost
nothing. When there is question of some
temporal concern we are all anxiety and
earnestness; nothing is suffered to impede
us; but when it is a matter that regards
the salvation of our soul, then all our en-
ergy is gone, we have no firmness of resolution, the veriest trifle gives an excuse for
omitting it. And yet attention to the affair
of our salvation is our one only important
concern; it alone can afford us any degree
of consolation in this life; it alone can
give us confidence at the moment of death;

regarding it alone will God demand an account of us when we appear before His judgment - seat; it alone can render us happy for eternity.

What is it that can afford us something of consolation amidst the trials and crosses of this life? One thing only—attending to the affair of our salvation, for then we shall have the hope that our crosses and trials will not go for nought, but that God will take them into account and recompense them one day in heaven.

What is that that can strengthen us against the fear of death, against the terrors of judgment, when our last moment arrives? Shall it be to recollect that we have been prosperous in life, that we have enjoyed its pleasures and gratified our passions? Oh, no; on the contrary, all that will then be to us only a new cause of regrets, fears, and alarm. What, then, can give us confidence at that terrible moment? One thing only—attention to our salvation, the having thought of it and laboured for it during life. And when we appear before God to be judged, about what shall we be interrogated? Concerning one thing only —the affair of our salvation. "Have you secured your salvation?" the strict, inexorable Judge will ask us. "Have you attended to it? have you laboured for it?" About this shall we be examined; and woe to us if we have neglected this all-important affair, for we shall then be condemned without mercy, and for eternity, to the most dreadful of all punishments. In fine, the affair of our salvation is the only thing that can render us happy during eternity. To what do all things earthly tend? To death, to the grave. One thing only can follow us into eternity—the affair of our salvation. Let us labour, then, for our salvation; let us do so with earnestness and zeal; let us labour for it to the end of our life, and heaven with all its joys shall be the recompense of our labours and our trials.

EXAMPLE.

The Grace of Salvation.

A prince of one of the reigning families of Germany had been reared in infidelity by an impious and depraved guardian. This irreligion which he had imbibed from the teachings of his master became more and more deeply rooted in his heart with his years. At the age of seventy-one no one could pronounce the name of God in his hearing

without the risk of having him give utterance to
blasphemies. A lady who knew him for twenty
years, touched by his unhappy state, recommended
him to the prayers of the Association of the Sacred
Heart of Mary. Some days later this man, who
hitherto had never had a pious thought, became
as if beside himself. It was grace that had begun
to work in him. On Sunday, the 14th of May, he
was again recommended to the prayers of the
Associates. Thenceforth he could rest neither
night nor day. If, overcome by fatigue and want
of sleep, he chanced to slumber for a moment, immediately a fearful dream awoke him in affright :
it seemed to him as if he was seized and dragged
before the judgment-seat of God, there to render
an account of his conduct. This thought pursued
him even in the day-time, and occasioned him
much suffering. Having at some time heard of
the extraordinary effects wrought in persons who
wore a miraculous medal of the Blessed Virgin, he
earnestly asked for one. A medal that had been
blessed and indulgenced was accordingly sent to
him. He received it with eagerness, kissed it re-
spectfully, and put it into his bosom, saying, " It
shall never leave me." On the Sunday following
prayers were again offered for him, and several
Communions were offered for his intention. From
that time peace was restored to his soul, and his
rest became sweet and tranquil. But the Blessed
Virgin, who desired his salvation, accorded him
much greater favours. One night he felt himself
awakened gently ; he opened his eyes and saw his
apartment filled with a brilliant light. Struck
with astonishment he sought an explanation of the

phenomenon, when a lady of noble, majestic mien, with a countenance full of sweetness and dignity, clothed in white, advanced towards him and said that it was time that he should cease to commit sin ; that if he died in his present state he should be lost for all eternity ; but if he became converted and approached the sacrament of penance, God would bestow a happiness upon him that should never end. At these words the lady disappeared, and all became dark again. Next night he was favoured with the same vision, and received the same warning ; and the same was repeated on the third night, but she added that she had come for the last time ; let him pay due attention to the advice she gave, for that his salvation depended upon it. She then disappeared, and he saw her no more. Vanquished by these wonders, he asked for a priest to instruct him in the Catholic religion, made his confession, received his first Communion on his seventy-second birth-day, and, completely changed under the miraculous care of Mary, became as gentle and humble as he had hitherto been arrogant and passionate. He wished to return to his native land in order to reanimate the faith of his fellow-countrymen by relating the favour he had received from the Blessed Virgin; but God was satisfied with his good intentions, and he died before the end of his journey (*Manuel de l'Archi-confrérie*).

PRACTICE.

We are on earth only to save our souls ; if that be not done, then all is lost to us. What will avail us all the goods of the world if we are damned ?

Of what use to have enjoyed pleasures here on
earth if we have to burn eternally in hell? Would
to heaven we were never born rather than that we
should be lost for all eternity!

EIGHTEENTH DAY.

SORROWS OF THE BLESSED VIRGIN AT THE FOOT OF THE CROSS.

MARY followed her Divine Son when He
ascended Calvary, and was present during
His last moments at the foot of the cross.
When a mother assists at the death of her
child, she tries to do all in her power to
mitigate the throes of his last agony; she
lavishes every care and attention on him;
she smoothes his pillow; she gives him re-
medies to lessen his sufferings; she evinces
her affection by locking him in her arms,
and bathing him with tears, and the poor
mother thus finds some solace in her trouble
and her sorrow.   But Mary on Calvary
had not this consolation; she beheld her
Son fastened to the cross, suspended between
heaven and earth, enduring the most dreadful torments, and she could not comfort
Him; she saw Him all bruised and covered

with wounds, and she could not stanch
the blood nor bind up His wounds; she
heard Him cry in desolation: "My God,
my God, why has Thou forsaken me?"
and she could not fly to His assistance;
she heard Him again exclaim: "I thirst!"
and she could not give Him a drop of water
to assuage His parching thirst; and not
only had she not the consolation of having
it in her power to comfort her beloved
Son, but she had the additional sorrow
to endure of seeing Him insulted and
outraged in the most inhuman manner.
She heard all the blasphemies, all the imprecations which they uttered against Him,
all the sacrilegious mockery which they
heaped upon Him; she saw His executioners exult in his sufferings, and drench
His mouth with vinegar even whilst He was
agonizing. Finally, Jesus expires on the
cross after three hours of dreadful torments,
and Mary has the added grief to see Him
outraged after death, to see His heart riven
with a spear. Oh, who could recount all the
agonies of Mary on Calvary at the death of
her Divine Son? Truly then was accomplished in her the prophecy of the venerable
Simeon, her maternal heart was transpierced

by a sword of sorrow. Every sigh of Jesus
on the cross, every outrage offered Him,
every blow, every wound that rent His
adorable body, were so many strokes of
the sword that pierced and lacerated the
heart of His tender Mother. No, never was
there sorrow like to that of Mary on Calvary.
She suffered more than all the martyrs
together, say the holy Fathers; therefore
has the Church styled her the Mother of
Sorrows, the Queen of Martyrs, titles which
she richly merited by all the sufferings
which she endured on Calvary at the foot
of the cross.

If we would be true Christians, let us
imitate Mary, let us follow Jesus to Calvary,
carrying our cross after Him. The cross
is the way to heaven, the way of the elect;
by that way have all the saints walked, and
even Jesus Christ Himself. He took up
His cross in the manger, in the stable at
Bethlehem, in being born in suffering and
poverty; and He carried it all His life-time
up to His death. Therefore, He only re-
cognises as His disciples those who carry
their cross after His example. "He that
taketh not up his cross," He says, "and
followeth me, is not worthy of me, cannot

be my disciple." We must then bear our cross if we would be disciples of Jesus Christ. Besides, in vain would we seek to avoid the cross, we shall meet it everywhere.

Whatever side we turn, wheresoever we abide, we shall always have to endure either bodily sufferings, or mental pain; and consequently we shall always have our cross to bear. It is found in every state and condition of life. Each has his own; no one is exempt. We sometimes repine at the weight of our cross; it seems to us that another would be more supportable, and that we could carry it with more courage; this is an error, an illusion. God knows best what is proportioned to our strength, and most suitable for us, and the cross that comes to us from His hands is sure to be the most profitable and useful for us. It is this that will sanctify us, provided only that we bear it with patience and resignation; for, to be holy, it is not enough that we have crosses, it is necessary, moreover, that we make a good use of them. Two men were on the cross on each side of Jesus on Calvary, the good and the bad thief. The former bore his sufferings patiently and with resignation, and he is

saved, Jesus promised that he should be
with Him in paradise. The other, on the
contrary, was impatient, murmured against
his fate, ceased not to give utterance to
blasphemies and imprecations, and he is
lost, and in hell. Let us, then, sanctify our
crosses by bearing them after Jesus, uniting them with that which our Divine Saviour has borne for love of us, and thus we
shall render them not only more meritorious,
but also more light and easy.

EXAMPLE.

Cure obtained through a Novena.

For many months, Sister St. Cecilia, a young
religious, languished on a bed of suffering. After
trying all the resources of their art, the physicians
declared her malady incurable. At first, a pain
commencing in the ankle of the right foot, spread
by degrees through the whole leg and side, sores
were formed all over her body, or rather it became
one general sore ; the flesh mortified, and exhaled
such an offensive odour, that even the sick person
herself was overcome and swooned from the effects
of it. She could not bear any nourishment: all
her support consisted of a biscuit steeped in water,
and even that she could not take without bringing
on a vomiting of blood. With all her dreadful
sufferings, she never uttered a complaint ; when

9

they became more intense than usual, she took her
crucifix, and pressed it to her lips, saying: "My
God, whatever Thou wilt; Thou hast borne much
more for me." On the approach of the feast of the
Immaculate Conception, 1855, the entire community resolved to perform a novena in honour of
the Blessed Virgin, in whom the invalid had the
most unbounded confidence. On the 7th December, the vigil of the feast, her sufferings increased,
at midnight they became unbearable, and in that
dreadful state she remained until two o'clock in
the morning. At two, the sick person, overcome
with fatigue and pain, fell into a deep sleep. Her
sleep, that before had been so disturbed, was calm
and peaceful. At six she still slept; it was the
hour of the Community Mass. They came to carry
her to the tribune of the chapel, where she was, according to custom, to receive Holy Communion;
when, behold! Mary had heard their prayers; she
was cured. She no longer felt the least pain; her
foot, leg, and side, were free from all swelling, the
livid colour had disappeared, her sores were completely healed, the infectious odour was gone, and
the blood once more circulated healthily through
the hitherto diseased parts, and restored to them
their natural heat. Her first word was one of
gratitude and love to Mary, her august benefactress. She at once arose from bed, took her
clothes and then without help proceeded to the
chapel. At the end of the corridor she perceived
the mother superior, and ran to her crying—
"Mother, mother, I am cured! the Blessed Virgin
has cured me!" The superior was filled with
emotion, in which the whole community soon

joined ; they repaired together to the chapel, where they prayed with renewed faith. Sister St. Cecilia took her place with them, heard Mass kneeling, communicated with the others, assisted at vespers and benediction, took her food with the sisters without experiencing any inconvenience, and joined in all the exercises of the house without feeling the least fatigue. The physician, struck with astonishment, was forced to acknowledge that this extraordinary cure was effected by the all-powerful hand of God (*Le Vœu National of Grenoble*).

PRACTICE.

Of whatever kind be the crosses that God sends us, let us receive them with submission, and bear them with patience and courage. Only on these conditions can we be accounted true Christians, and thus only will Jesus Christ recognise us as his true disciples; in a word, it is by fulfilling these conditions that we can hope one day to enter heaven.

NINETEENTH DAY.

JOY OF THE BLESSED VIRGIN AT THE RESURRECTION OF HER DIVINE SON.

ALTHOUGH the Gospel does not relate that our Saviour manifested Himself to his Holy

yet we cannot reasonably doubt that it was
so. The love He had for this tender mother,
the respect He entertained for her, the
reverence He had ever evinced towards her,
all tend to make us believe that He hastened to visit her, to console her in her
troubles and her sorrow. She had been
with Him on Calvary; she had shared all the
sufferings and ignominies of His Passion;
it was, therefore, most just that she should
first participate in the joy of His resurrection. What, then, must have been her joyful
delight when she beheld her beloved Son
arisen, clad in glory and immortality!
What sweet intercourse, what holy com-
munings during these forty days that she
had still the happiness of passing with Him
on earth! How fully was she solaced for
all the cruel anguish which she had endured
on Calvary! Thus does God ever proportion His graces and consolations to the trials
and sufferings which we bear for His sake.

Great though the joy of Mary was, yet,
like all the joys of earth, it was of but
short duration. . On the fortieth day after
his Resurrection, Jesus, accompanied by His
Holy Mother and his apostles, proceeded to
Mount Olivet, and there, in their presence,

and having bestowed upon them His last
benediction, He ascended into heaven, and
there took possession of a throne of glory
on the right hand of God His Father. Oh!
who can recount the sentiments of Mary,
when she was constrained to part from her
beloved Son and receive His last farewell.
How she would have wished to be able to
accompany Him and ascend with Him to
heaven to share His happiness and glory.
Consequently, though her body still remained on earth, it may be said that her
heart and her soul went up to heaven with
Jesus. Wholly detached from the things
of this world, she sighed only for the possession of the goods of eternity. Thither
all her thoughts, all her desires, all her
affections were directed.

After the example of Mary, let us hold
ourselves detached from the things of earth,
and aspire only after the true and solid
goods of eternity. What, in fact, is there
that should attach us to this life? This
life that is so full of misery and tribulations, its goods so uncertain, its honours
only a vapour, its pleasures so momentary
and leaving but regret and remorse after
them. And even if the goods of this life

were real, as they are in truth only false
and deceitful, what would remain to us of
them at death? how much of them could
we bring with us to the other world?
Nothing, absolutely nothing; nothing shall
accompany us thither except our vices and
our virtues, our sins and our good works;
we shall bring nothing thither but the joy
and the peace of a good conscience, if we
have lived well, or the bitter sorrow and
regret of having lost our souls, if we have
lived badly. Yes, though we should have
been during life the poorest and most unfortunate of men, if we save our soul and
gain heaven we are most happy; it is all
gain and success for us. For all eternity
we shall be encompassed with the most
ineffable happiness and delights. On the
other hand, though we should have enjoyed all the good things, all the honours
and pleasures possible here below, if we
have neglected our salvation and lost our
soul, we are supremely unhappy; everything is lost to us and lost for ever. For
all eternity we shall be a prey to the most
dreadful sufferings and the most unbearable torments. Insensate then, a thousand
times insensate, he who thinks only of the

perishable things of this life, and allows
his affections to be absorbed by that which
must soon be left behind, that which death
will quickly snatch from him, and ne-
glects the salvation of his soul, the only
true and solid pursuit that can render him
eternally happy in heaven !

EXAMPLE.

Sacrifice for the Faith.

In March, 1842, a young man presented himself
to M. Desgenettes, curé of Notre Dame des Victoires, Paris. He was about twenty-five years of
age, in tattered garments, almost barefoot, yet
there was perceptible about him something that
indicated high rank. " What would you with
me, my friend ? " said M. Desgenettes. " Mon-
sieur, I am a Russian ; I come from Varsovia."
" And why have you come to Paris ? " " I am a
Catholic, and I have fled to Paris, because they
were about to persecute me to make me renounce
my religion." This young man was in truth the
son of a Russian prince attached to the person of
the Emperor. His family, who designed him for
a diplomatic career, had given him a brilliant education. Already for some years he had occupied
a position in the Government of Varsovia, when a
Catholic lady put into his hands The Manual
and the Annals of the Confraternity of the Sacred
Heart of Mary. He read them with interest ; his
eyes were opened, he saw the error in which he had

been reared, and became convinced that the Catholic was the only true religion. He accordingly
abjured the Greek schism and was received into
the true Church. For a year he had professed
himself a Catholic, and lived in the strict fulfilment of his religious duties, when suddenly one
day a friend came hastily into his office and said:
"Sergius, do you know what is about to take
place?" "What?" "The Government have determined to arrest you forthwith, and conduct you
under escort to St. Petersburg, because you are a
Catholic. One who has seen you communicate at
the church of the Dominicans has betrayed you."
Struck with terror at the thought of the horrible
persecution which he knew he should have to endure, the young prince immediately left his office,
fled from Varsovia, and on foot, without passport
or money, he directed his course towards the
Church of our Lady of Victories, at Paris. "She
is my mother," he said to himself; "to her I owe
my conversion, and she will be my help in my misfortune." In this hope, and having changed clothes
with a poor countryman, the better to cover his
flight, he traversed Poland, Prussia, and France,
travelling twenty leagues a day, and stopping only
to take a little rest at night in an outhouse and
frequently in the open fields; finally he reached
Paris, and prostrated himself before the statue of
Our Lady of Victories, thanking his august protectress for having preserved him from persecution for his faith; but unknown and without
means, what was to become of him? Mary, in
whom he placed his trust, did not desert him.
She inspired him with the thought of presenting

himself to M. Desgenettes, who full of admiration
for the courage and virtue of the pious young man,
placed him in a religious house. There he spent
some time considering his vocation, and then decided on embracing the ecclesiastical state, in
order to devote himself to the foreign missions.
Thus did this young nobleman, rich, talented, and
highly accomplished, sacrifice his fortune and his
earthly prospects, abandon family and country,
renounce all the honours, pleasures, and goods of
this world, to save his soul and preserve his faith.
What an example for us who are so tardy in
making the least sacrifice for the salvation of our
souls! (*Extract from the Archives de l'Archicon-
frérie.*)

PRACTICE.

Call to mind the nothingness and short-lived
nature of the things of this life. Alas! how are
we blinded! We attach ourselves to the perishable goods of this life that will so soon slip
through our hands, and we forget eternity, that
dread eternity upon which we shall enter perhaps
to-morrow. Where is our reason? Where is our
faith?

TWENTIETH DAY.

THE LAST YEARS OF THE BLESSED VIRGIN.

ACCORDING to the most commonly received
opinion, Mary lived nearly twenty-three

many years have we already passed on
earth? And are we on that account more
perfect and more virtuous? Time flies
rapidly, and presently we shall find ourselves unexpectedly come to the end of our
career. Oh! let us not waste time that is so
short and precious. The bitterest regret of
the lost souls is to have misused time. If it
were permitted them to return to life, how
they would profit of the opportunity to do
penance, to labour for their salvation! But
that opportunity, that shall never be given
to the damned, God gives to us; we have
time still at our disposal. Let us turn it
to account to secure our salvation, to prepare ourselves against the time when we
shall have to appear before that dread tribunal, where we shall have to render an
account of all our thoughts, all our words,
all our actions. We should be terrified to
have to give a rigorous account of a single
day; what then shall it be to account for
so many months, so many years, for a long
lifetime? Even Job, that just man, trembled when he thought of the judgment of
God. "What shall I do," he exclaims,
"when God shall rise to judge? and when

he shall examine, what shall I answer
him?" (Job, xxxi. 14).

If the just man shall scarcely be saved,
as St. Peter says, what shall become of the
sinner and the wicked? The way by
which we shall be prepared to appear with
confidence before God in judgment is to
anticipate it, and judge ourselves now, and
to say often to ourselves : Would I be content to appear before the judgment seat of
God after doing this act, after uttering this
word, after dwelling upon this thought,
after consenting to this desire?

EXAMPLE.

A Young Girl Interred Alive.

The person of whom we speak was called Juliet,
and was employed as lady's maid to a duchess.
Without altogether losing her faith, she amused
herself, after the example of her mistress, by turning
into ridicule the ceremonies and most sacred mysteries of our holy religion. She fancied that in
acting thus, she should be regarded as a person of
courage and strong mind, as if there could be courage and strong-mindedness in mocking God and
his saints. They found her one day, dead and
cold in her bed. The physician was brought, at-
tested the fact of her death, and next day at nine
o'clock in the morning she was buried. The un-

happy girl, however, had only fallen into a le-
thargy, and the same day towards evening, having
recovered her consciousness, what was her astonishment to find herself enveloped and bound in a
sheet so that she could not move! She made an
effort to free herself, but in vain; she found herself hemmed in on every side between four planks.
"Where am I?" she cried, "have they thought me
dead and buried me?" She cried aloud, but no one
heard her; she listened, but no sound struck her
ear; she looked, but saw nothing but a dark and
frightful night; she could no longer doubt she
was in a tomb, laid amongst the dead. There was
she to end her existence, without help or consolation, in slow and dreadful agony. This thought
sent a chill of fear through her frame; but, presently, a far more terrible thought presented
itself to her mind; she called to mind the sins of
her past life, her blasphemies, her impious and
sacrilegious mocking of holy things; she saw God
ready to judge her, hell yawning to engulf her, and
the devils eager to drag her to torments. A cold
sweat bathed her whole body. "O my God," she
exclaimed, "pardon me my sins; I am heartily
sorry for them; would that I could blot them out
with my blood! Holy Virgin, the refuge of sinners,
help of the afflicted, come to my help, take me out

hearing her cries, set himself to open the grave. There he found her on her bier, her body all torn and bloody, her hair scattered about, and the winding-sheet rent and displaced. As soon as he loosed her to ascertain if she still lived, she heaved a deep sigh, opened her eyes, made an effort to arise, and cried out—"O my God, I thank thee!" They bestowed on her all the care that her state required, and in a few days she was almost quite restored to health. She recounted all she had undergone during the long hours she had been in the tomb; then after dividing between the grave-digger and the poor all the money she possessed, she entered a convent of the Ursulines, there to do penance for the sins of her past life, and to prepare herself to appear before the dread judgment-seat of God, to which she had already been so near (*Sabatier De Castres*).

PRACTICE.

Often call to mind that terrible judgment where we shall have to render an account of all our thoughts, words, and actions. Surely, if even the saints trembled in contemplating this fearful judgment, we have reason to tremble at it! Let us prepare for this judgment by judging ourselves severely, and by leading an edifying and Christian life.

TWENTY-FIRST DAY.

DEATH OF THE BLESSED VIRGIN.

AT length the moment drew nigh when all the desires of the Blessed Virgin were to be accomplished, when that tender mother was to leave this valley of tears to be united for ever to her Divine Son in heaven. It is related that some days' before her death, an angel appeared to her, holding a palm-branch, and announced to her the termination of her exile. How full of joy she must have been at this happy announcement. How earnestly did she thank the Lord for it! The moment of her death being come, she consoled the faithful who pressed around her, she encouraged them to perseverance, promised to be their advocate and protectress in heaven as she had been their mother and their refuge on earth, and having imparted to them her blessing, she resigned her soul into the hands of her Son, and slept peacefully on the bosom of the Lord. It was neither the effects of sickness nor the decay of nature, nor the decrepitude of age, although she died at an advanced age, that severed the bonds which held her soul united to her body, it was solely the fire of divine love. All aflame with this sacred fire, her beautiful soul detached itself, without an effort, from her virginal body, and was transported in triumph into heaven, even to the foot of the throne of the Eternal. Such was the precious death of the Blessed Virgin. Oh! would that ours might be in anywise like to hers! But, let us remember that to die a holy death like Mary, we must live holily like her; for a happy death is the recompense of a good life.

Although God had, by a special privilege, preserved Mary from original sin, He willed not to preserve her from the death of the body, which is the penalty of that sin; He, on the contrary, willed that she should undergo it, like the other children of Adam, to show that the sentence of death is universal and irrevocable; to render her also the more conformable to her Divine Son, who, very God that He was, still would submit, through love for us, to the most humiliating death, to the death of the cross; finally, the Blessed Virgin died to teach us by her example how we ought to dispose ourselves for our last moment. Mary's

whole life was a preparation for death.
From the first dawn of reason to her last
sigh, she never ceased to dispose herself for
it by an angelical purity, by detachment
from creatures, by an ardent love of God,
and by the practice of every virtue. Thus
death had nothing painful or sorrowful for
her. Full of a tender confidence and burning with the desire to be united to Jesus
Christ, her Divine Son, she passed tran-
quilly from this mortal life to the possession of a happy eternity, as one falls into a
gentle sleep.

Like Mary, we should continually prepare ourselves for death. This was the
occupation of all the saints whilst on earth;
they did nothing else than prepare themselves to die well; and, after passing long
years in tears, fasting and penance, they
feared that they had still not done enough.
And what are we doing towards preparing
for that terrible moment which will decide
our eternal lot? Everything, in fact, depends on the moment of death. If we die
in the state of grace, we are secure of being
eternally happy; if, on the contrary, we
die in the state of mortal sin, we shall be
miserable, accursed, reprobates for eternity.

Oh! let us not await the moment of death
to prepare ourselves for it: it will be then
too late, but let us prepare for it all our
days. Let us pass each day as if it was the
last of our life; let us frequently examine
our conscience to ascertain if we be in a
state to appear before God; let us often say
to ourselves: If death occurred to me now,
should I be well prepared? should I have
nothing to reproach myself with? Would
I be content to die in my present state?
If our conscience be not at peace, if it
reproach us with some fault with which we
would not be satisfied to appear before the
tribunal of God, let us hasten to extricate
ourself from that state by having recourse
to the Sacrament of Penance; let us never
rest contentedly in sin, for death may surprise us at any moment. We cannot count
on youth, nor strength, nor health; death
occurs at every age. "Be you always
ready," Jesus Christ says to us, "for you
know not the day nor the hour. At what
hour you think not, the Son of man will
come."

EXAMPLE.

St. Francis De Sales delivered from temptation through the Intercession of the Blessed Virgin

St. Francis De Sales, at the age of seventeen, was at Paris for the completion of his studies, when God allowed him to experience a trial the most painful to a tender and loving soul such as his. The devil endeavoured to persuade him that all he did for God was useless, as his reprobation was inevitable. God, who wished to teach him from personal experience the compassion that should be felt for those similarly tempted, seemed as if He abandoned him and left him a prey to the assaults of hell. In this impenetrable night, no ray of divine light reached him, no consoling thought came to give him comfort. In vain he implored heaven for help; heaven appeared as if closed against him, and his God seemed as if deaf to his prayers. No more hope of one day possessing that infinite beauty which heretofore had been the dearest object of his desires, hell alone presented itself to him with its dreadful eternal solitude, where God is never seen; where there can be no love of Him; where on the contrary, the heart abhors and hates Him, and the mouth blasphemes Him without ceasing! Francis could not contain himself at the thought of this; he lost his appetite and rest, and his health visibly declined. The freshness and beauty of his countenance faded away like a lily which a poisonous wind has breathed upon and withered; his eyes became sunken, and he was reduced almost to a skeleton. There was no more that amiable playfulness that

had made him so engaging to all who knew him;
the society of even his nearest friends was dis-
tasteful ; absent and care-worn in mind, he sought
for solitude, which, when he found it, only tended
to make his sorrow the more unendurable. If he
thought of opening his heart to some friend, the
load indeed would have been lightened, but the
shame of the avowal closed his lips even with
regard to his tutor, who loved him tenderly, and
who asked him in vain the cause of this sad change.
He continued nearly a month in this state, excit-
ing the pity of all, and causing the utmost anxiety
to his friends. A little time more and the young
Francis would have died; but God, satisfied with
having proved him, inspired him with the thought
of going to the Church of Notre-Dame-des-Gres,
where he had before made his vow of chastity,
and the first object on which his eyes rested was
the statue of the Blessed Virgin. At sight of it,
a feeling of confidence sprung up anew in his
aflicted heart ; he cast himself at Mary's feet, and
looking upon himself as all unworthy of directly
addressing God, he besought her to obtain for him
of God's mercy the favour that if he was so unfortunate as to hate Him in the other life, he
might be allowed to love Him with all his heart in
this ; he then recited the *Memorare*, shedding a
torrent of tears. This touching petition, so far
removed from the dispositions of a reprobate,
moved the heart of Mary to compassion, and
Francis at once experienced the happy effect of
the protection of her whom the Church with so
much justice styles the Comforter of the Afflicted.
Hardly had he ended his prayer than he felt as it

were a mountain removed from his heart ; a gentle
light dissipated the cloud that had enveloped his
soul, joy and delight succeeded to black grief, he
quite recovered his cheerfulness, his health returned, and from that day forth the peace which
he had obtained through the Blessed Virgin was
never disturbed.

PRACTICE.

Think often that we shall soon have to die. Yet,
a few years, perhaps but a few days, and all shall
be over with us ; we shall have rendered our account to God, and our eternal lot shall have been
decided. O moment of death, how terrible art
thou ! I will think of it, I will prepare myself for it.

TWENTY-SECOND DAY.

THE ASSUMPTION OF THE BLESSED VIRGIN.

AFTER her death, Mary was wrapped in a
shroud and placed in the tomb, but she
remained not long there ; for, according to
the universal belief, she arose 'after the
example of her Divine Son, on the third
day, glorious and triumphant from the dead.
A venerable tradition handed down to us
age to age, from the time of the
tles, informs us that the body of the

Blessed Virgin was carried to Gethsemani, and there interred amidst the chants of the angels and the apostles; that during three successive days delightful music was heard in the air; and that on the third day, the chanting having ceased, St. Thomas, the only one of the apostles who had not assisted at the death and burial of the Mother of God, having arrived at Jerusalem, earnestly begged to be allowed once more to contemplate and venerate her who had borne the Saviour of mankind. Yielding to his entreaties the apostles opened the tomb, but the body was no longer there; they found in it only the shroud and drapery in which the body had been wrapped, and which shed around a sweet odour. Struck with astonishment at the sight of this mystery, the apostles reclosed the tomb, convinced that the Divine Word, who had vouchsafed to become incarnate in the immaculate womb of Mary, had not permitted her chaste body to be subject to corruption, but had raised it to life and transported it to heaven, to be at once admitted to a participation of her beatitude and glory. Yes, it is the unanimous belief of the Church that the Blessed Virgin was assumed both body- and soul into heaven. It is not an article of faith, but yet it is a truth so universally acknowledged, that to call it in question would be an act of the greatest temerity.

God would grant this glorious privilege to Mary to render her the more conformable to her Divine Son, who remained Himself but three days in the grave; and also to recompense her inviolable purity, preserved unstained to the end; this privilege was accorded her to honour her virginal body, become by the Incarnation of the Word, the sanctuary of grace, and the temple of the Divinity; and finally God bestowed this favour upon her to give us in the resurrection of His Holy Mother, an assured pledge of our own future resurrection.

It is an undoubted truth that we shall rise again one day. All, great and small, the just and the sinner, all shall reassume the same bodies which we now have, and shall appear both body and soul before the tribunal of the sovereign judge. And if, by virtues and good works, we have ted to be of the number of the just, nly shall our soul be happy and glorified for all eternity in heaven, but our body also shall share in its glory and beatitude. On the contrary, if we be so unhappy as to be numbered with the reprobate, not only shall our soul be condemned to suffer eternally in hell, but our body also shall share in its sorrows and sufferings, as it had partaken during life in its guilty and criminal pleasures. "The hour cometh," says Jesus Christ (John, v. 28, 29), "wherein all that are in the graves shall hear the voice of the Son of God. And they that have done good things, shall come forth unto the resurrection of life, but they that have done evil, unto the resurrection of judgment." Oh! since our body is destined to arise again one day, let us ever hold it in respect and never sully it by sin. We venerate the temples of God, and would shudder to profane them. But "Know you not," says St. Paul (1 Cor. 6, 19,) "that your members are the temple of the Holy Ghost?" and "if any man violate the temple of God; him shall God destroy" (1 Cor. iii. 17). And again the same Apostle says (1 Cor. vi. 15), "Your bodies are the members of Christ." What horrible profanation that of making the members of Jesus Christ the instru-

ments of crime and iniquity! Let us then
keep our bodies free from all sin, from all
impurity, that on the day of general resurrection they may arise glorious from the
grave, and be admitted to participate in the
joy which the bodies of the just shall
possess in heaven.

EXAMPLE.

*Devotion of St. Stanislaus Kostka to the Blessed
Virgin; how it was rewarded.*

From the most tender age, St. Stanislaus Kostka
had a great devotion to the Blessed Virgin which
increased with his years. During his noviciate in
the Society of Jesus, he made it his special study
to become acquainted with those sayings of the
saints and passages in their writings that treated
of the praises of Mary, and that were most cal-
culated to give a high idea of her power and
greatness. He had also a custom, at the commencement of each action, to turn in the direction
of a church dedicated to the Blessed Virgin, in
order to ask her blessing. Mary, in return for this
filial love, bestowed on the young Stanislaus the
precious gift of an angelical purity; if he heard
an expression of an indelicate nature he forthwith
swooned away. He was sure to obtain all that he
asked through the intercession of the Blessed
Virgin, both for himself and for his fellow novices,
who had come to understand the efficacy of his
prayers.

Before he joined the Society of Jesus he fell
dangerously ill, and seemed on the point of death.
He had received the Holy Viaticum through the
ministry of angels, having asked in vain for the
attendance of a priest in the house of a Protestant
where he happened to be lodging. He awaited
only his last moment, when of a sudden he was
favoured with a heavenly vision; he beheld the
Blessed Virgin approach him with a countenance
of inexpressible sweetness, bearing in her arms the
infant Jesus. She addressed Stanislaus in words
of the utmost tenderness, consoled and encouraged
him; then placing her Son upon the bed she
allowed Stanislaus to caress Him. Stanislaus was
so transported with joy that he would not have
relinquished his hold of the Divine infant; but
Mary withdrew Him saying: "My son, your hour
is not yet come; you must merit the possession of
Jesus by faithful obedience to His will." She
then disappeared, leaving Stanislaus so much im-
proved, that he was soon in a condition to go to a
church to thank God for the favour he had
received.

In his last illness Stanislaus was favoured with
another vision of the Blessed Virgin. He had long
desired to die on the feast of the Assumption, and
had implored this holy mother to obtain for him
this grace. His prayer was heard. He was seized
with a fever, and five days before this feast he was
so ill that he had the last Sacraments administered
to him. After receiving the Holy Viaticum and
having invoked the intercession of the saints, he
gave himself to silence and recollection; then it
was that Mary came to seek her child and to con-

duct him to Jesus. She appeared to him surrounded by a numerous retinue of virgins, clad in robes of dazzling whiteness. " Come with us, Stanislaus," she said to him ; " it is time to quit this land of sorrow ; come to share with us the eternal joys." At these words he expired, and his innocent soul ascended to heaven to enjoy during eternity the society of Jesus and Mary.

PRACTICE.

We shall all rise again on the last day ; this is an article of faith ; the resurrection shall be an occasion of joy and consolation for the just, but one of terror and consternation for sinners. Which shall it be for us? Let us examine our conduct and reflect.

___

TWENTY-THIRD DAY.

CROWNING OF THE BLESSED VIRGIN IN HEAVEN.

MARY entered heaven not like the other saints ; she entered it as Mother of God and as queen of angels and saints. All paradise was moved on her arrival; the whole heavenly court advanced to meet her, to felicitate her, and to render her their homage as to their sovereign. Jesus Christ himself came to receive her, he put her

in possession of her glorious throne on His
right hand ; he placed upon her brow the
double crown of virgins and of martyrs;
he put a sceptre into her hand and said :
Reign, O My Mother ! reign eternally
over the angels and saints, and all creatures.
Behold my graces and my treasures; I
place them at your disposal.   Bestow them
upon your clients, your children, and your
faithful servants.   Then was accomplished
in heaven the prodigy of which St. John
speaks in the Apocalypse : " A great sign
appeared in heaven ; a woman clothed with
the sun and the moon under her feet, and on
her head a crown of twelve stars" (Apoc. xii.
1).   This wonderful woman invested with
such splendour, is the Blessed Virgin,
crowned by her Divine Son, queen of angels
and of men. Behold now this humble virgin.
this poor mother, lately so despised and
slighted upon earth, so deluged in sorrows
on Calvary, so persecuted during life,
behold her now in the bosom of God, surrounded with honour, disposing at pleasure
the treasures of heaven, seated upon a throne
the most elevated in heaven, next to that
of her Divine Son, and none but the Divinity itself above her.   What glory for Mary

to find herself thus powerful and exalted!
What consolation for us! for we know that
the more powerful and exalted she is in
heaven, the greater is her compassion for
her unhappy children on earth, the greater
is her desire to bestow upon us marks of
a tender parent's love. But how has Mary
attained to this height of glory and power?
By her fidelity to grace and by the practice
of every virtue. Let us, then, imitate this
blessed mother, let us practise the virtues
which she practised on earth, and then we
shall, one day, share in her glory and beatitude in heaven.

Yes, we are all called to reign hereafter
with Mary in heaven; but to reach that
blessed abode we must strive and labour
for it. Heaven is a recompense, therefore
it must be merited; it is a crown, therefore it must be won; it is a kingdom,
therefore it must be conquered. "The
kingdom of heaven suffereth violence, and
the violent bear it away" (Matt. xi., 12).
This is the prize for which the saints suffered, the thought of which urged and
cheered them on to victory. They "had
trials of mockeries and stripes, moreover,
also of bonds and prisons; they were stoned,

they were cut asunder, they were tempted,
they were put to death by the sword"
(Heb. xi., 36, 37). Others wandered " in
deserts, in mountains and in dens, and in
caves of the earth" (ibid. v. 38), having no
other food than roots and wild fruits; others
were loaded with chains, clothed in hair-
cloth, had their bodies tortured, and watered
the earth with their tears and their blood.
Behold what the saints have done and suffered to get to heaven. And what have
we done hitherto for this end? Where are
our struggles and our victories? Where
our works of penance and mortification?
No doubt it is hard to wage a continual
war on self. "But if the labour affright
you," says St. Augustine, "let the recompense encourage you." This recompense
shall be great and magnificent beyond expression. "The eye hath not seen," says
St. Paul (1 Cor. ii. 9), nor ear heard,
neither hath it entered into the heart of
man, what things God hath prepared for
them that love Him." There "death shall
be no more, nor mourning, nor crying, nor
sorrow" (Apoc. xxi. 4). There there shall
be happiness infinite, unalterable, and unending; there shall our heart be fully sa-

tisfied, all our desires perfectly realised; there all shall be joy supreme and all satisfying, secured for all eternity.

EXAMPLE.

The Sceptre of Mary.

The seminary of Sables-d'Olonne, in the diocese of Luçon, was placed in an especial manner under the protection of the Blessed Virgin; it had chosen her as its mistress and sovereign, and in that quality had made her an offering of a silver sceptre, as a symbol of royalty. This seminary had been some years thus placed under the special guardianship of Mary, when, on the 27th December, 1835, at about two o'clock in the morning, the entire community were aroused from sleep by the cries of "Fire! fire!" We can readily imagine the tumult and confusion caused amongst the pupils and other inmates on finding the building in flames. Some ran to save their effects; others to seek refuge from the fire; others again ran into the town to alarm the inhabitants, and summon them to their aid. The darkness of night, the lurid glow of the conflagration, the clanging of the tocsin sounding for help, the clamour that was constantly on the increase, all tended to add to this scene of desolation. The whole town turned out to rescue their seminary from destruction: but already the fire had destroyed three apartments and had seized on the timber work of the pavilion situate on the north. To add to the misfortune, there were neither the appliances nor a sufficient supply of water at hand to extinguish the flames. And, moreover, the wind blew violently from the north, and sent showers of sparks from the burning pavilion on to the main portion of the building. In vain did the intrepid workmen mount the blazing walls, exposing themselves to danger of death in order to prevent the fire from extending; all their heroic efforts were unavailing. The entire seminary would infallibly have become a prey to the flames, when, by an inspiration from heaven, the superior ran to the statue of the Blessed Virgin, fell on his knees before it, reminded Mary that she was the queen and mistress of the house, and supplicated her to come to their assistance. He then arose full of confidence, took the Sceptre of Mary in his hand, and cast it into the midst of the flames, where they burned with the greatest violence. Never was faith more promptly recompensed; on the instant the wind changed, and bore the flames in an opposite direction; presently they got the fire under control and the seminary was saved. One of the first cares was to search for the sceptre, though with little hope of being successful. What was their delight to find it at length, quite uninjured, and only sullied by the fire. The community entered into an engagement to observe a solemn procession for three years on the anniversary of the event in honour of the Blessed Virgin, and as an act of thankful recognition of her maternal assistance; and a picture was designed, representing the building in flames, and the Queen of Heaven arresting the fire by waving her sceptre in the direction (*Michaud*).

11

PRACTICE.

We can all aspire to heaven, and are called to it; but in order to attain to it, we must labour for it and merit it; we must fight our way to it and win it; for the kingdom of heaven suffereth violence, and it is only those who exercise a holy violence over their evil propensities that can hope to bear away the prize.

———

TWENTY-FOURTH DAY.

PROFOUND HUMILITY OF THE BLESSED VIRGIN.

THAT which Jesus Christ says of himself may be also applied to his most holy mother —"Learn of me, because I am meek and humble of heart" (Matt. xi. 29). Yes, Mary was ever truly humble in heart and mind. Her whole life was a constant exercise of the virtue of humility. The more it pleased God to exalt her and load her with favours, the more did she study to be lowly and humble. An angel was sent to announce to her that she was chosen to be the mother of the Saviour, and so far from being elated by the glorious announcement, she replied with humility: "Behold the handmaid of the Lord." The angel told her that she was " full of grace," and " blessed amongst women,' and she was troubled at his words, his praises gave the alarm to her humility. "She would never have been troubled," says St. Bernardine, " if the angel had told her that she was wicked and a sinner."

In her quality of Mother of God, Mary might justly claim the respect and homage not only of men but also of angels and saints; and yet, without a thought of her eminent dignity, she set out in haste to visit her cousin Elizabeth; she was the first to salute her and humbly to offer her services. Therefore it was that, filled with astonishment at her readiness and modesty, Elizabeth exclaimed in admiration : " Whence is this to me, that the Mother of my Lord should come to me?" (Luke i. 43).

At Bethlehem, at the birth of Jesus, Mary saw herself repulsed and despised; but far from complaining of it or being offended at it, she, on the contrary, took occasion from it to abase and humble herself the more. Behold her again in the temple on the day of her Purification.

What modesty! what humility! She knew
that in giving birth to the Son of God she
had contracted no stain, and still she goes
through the form of Purification as if she
had been impure; she knew that she was
the Mother of the Eternal, of the All-
mighty, and yet she identifies herself with
ordinary mothers; she was the Queen
of Heaven, and contents herself with
making the offering of the poor. She avoids
with care all that could distinguish her in
the eyes of men. She sought not to appear or to be elevated above others; she, on
the contrary, sought only the lowest place,
and to remain unnoticed and unknown.
But it was not outwardly only that Mary
showed herself meek and humble; she was
so much more in the very depths of her
heart; for it is in the heart that true and
solid humility is to be found. She not only
submitted willingly, to contempt and humiliations, she even desired and sought
them; she was, in a word, the most humble
of all creatures; and for that reason it was,
say the Holy Fathers, that she was raised
to the sublime dignity of Mother of God.
How far removed are we from these holy
dispositions of Mary!

ment, and we think but of how we shall
obtain notoriety and human applause. And
all the time what have we to be proud of ?
" What hast thou," says St. Paul (1 Cor.
iv. 7), " that thou hast not received ? And
if thou hast received, why dost thou
glory ?" In truth, what have we of our
own but sin, misery, and nothingness ?
" Wherefore, God resisteth the proud and
giveth grace to the humble" (James, iv. 6).
But in proportion as pride is hateful to
God, so is humility pleasing in his sight.
Humility is a virtue so precious in the esteem of God, that Jesus Christ himself came
down from heaven to teach it to us. " Learn
of me," He says, " because I am meek and
humble of heart." And not content to
teach us this virtue by His words, He in-
structs us in it by His own example : He
is humility itself; He annihilated Himself;
He suffered injuries, insults, and calumnies; He died the most ignominious of
deaths. Humility is so indispensable a
virtue, that without it we cannot be saved.
"Unless you become as little children,"
says our Saviour, " you shall not enter into
the kingdom of heaven" (Matt. xviii. 3).
Let us then, ever, think lowly of ourselves,

by bearing in mind that we are nought but
weakness and misery, but dust and ashes;
let us accept willingly every humiliation
that God sends us; let us not pride ourselves
on our riches, talents, or endowments; let
us never despise any one, but always think
others better than we are; finally, let us,
like Mary, study to be humble and to shun
the vain applause of the world, and God,
who delights to raise up the humble and
lowly, will give us a high place in his eternal
kingdom.

EXAMPLE.

Pride vanquished.

A certain lawyer, aged thirty-two, had naturally
a fiery and overbearing disposition; but in place
of combating the spirit of pride that possessed such
dominion over him, he, on the contrary, fostered
and flattered it. Thus this sad propensity had become to him an occasion of continual trouble and
torment. He could not brook the slightest contra-
diction; the merest trifle put him in a rage.
One day, having set his heart upon the attainment
of a certain object, he met with an insurmountable
obstacle that frustrated the accomplishment of his
desires. He became as if delirious with anger, he
shed tears of passion, and his whole frame trembled
violently. Being thus unable to proceed on his
way, he sought some place where he could rest.
It was about three o'clock in the evening, and the

church of Notre Dame des Victoires was at hand.
He entered, and found it empty ; he advanced to
the chapel of the Blessed Virgin and cast himself
on his knees, though not at all through devotion.
Looking up to the statue of the Blessed Virgin, he
cried out in an impious tone : "You who are called
the Consoler of the Afflicted, help me if you have the
power to do so." Mary deigned to hear this
prayer, all-unworthy though it was. Scarcely had
he spoken, when he felt his trouble and agitation
greatly diminished. Presently he was seized with
a new access of passion; and again, and a third
time did he address himself to the Blessed Virgin.
"You who are the consolation of the unhappy," he
said, "look with pity on me." After remaining
nearly an hour in the church, he returned home ;
but what was his astonishment to find on the
mantelpiece of his chamber the *Imitation of Christ.*
He knew that he was not possessed of a copy of
this book, and no one could have placed it there
in his absence, as he had locked his door when
going out, and had taken the key with him. He
took up the mysterious volume, and opening it at
random, read these words: "In what things a man
has more sinned, in those shall he be more heavily
punished." He was struck with this sentence, and
applied it to himself. What, he said, was the
cause of the tortures I endured to-day? It was
my pride, and I was punished in that by which I.
had the more sinned. He paused a little, and then
taking up the book and opening it as before, he
read: "It is by resisting his passions, and not in
becoming their slave, that a man shall find true
peace of heart." These words were to him as if a

warning from heaven. He at once resolved to combat and conquer his pride. For that end he continued to implore the aid of the Blessed Virgin, and by means of prayer and determined efforts, he completely succeeded, and became as humble and gentle as he had heretofore been proud and imperious.

Like this young man, let us ask the assistance of Mary in conquering our evil propensities, and we shall surely triumph if we pray with perseverance, and make the necessary efforts for that end (*Manuel de l'Archiconfrerie*).

PRACTICE.

Let us be ever humble and gentle, accepting willingly such humiliations as happen to us; repressing the feelings of self-love that spring up in our heart; subduing irritability and testiness, which are the fruits of pride; bearing patiently to be told of our faults, and applying ourselves to their correction.

TWENTY-FIFTH DAY.

FIRM AND UNFALTERING FAITH OF THE BLESSED VIRGIN.

As the humility of the Blessed Virgin was profound and sincere, so was her faith proportionately firm and unfaltering. With

humble simplicity she believed truths even
the most difficult of belief. An angel, on
the part of God, announces to her the most
unheard, the most inconceivable of mysteries; he announces to her that she is to
become the Mother of the Eternal, the
Omnipotent. Undoubtedly, Mary did not
understand this mystery; still at the word
of the angel she believed without hesitation,
because she knew that God can neither
deceive nor be deceived, and that when He
proposes a truth to us, we should believe it
without reasoning upon it, even when it
exceeds our feeble intelligence.

When the time of her delivery was come,
Mary brought forth her Divine Infant at
Bethlehem, born in a poor stable; she beheld Him feeble, suffering, and subject to
the like miseries and needs as other children;
and yet, despite this poverty and apparent
weakness, she recognised Him as her Saviour and her God. She saw Him for
thirty years living in the greatest obscurity, performing nothing remarkable or
extraordinary; she saw Him employed as a
simple mechanic, a poor artizan; and still,
notwithstanding this life of obscurity and
retirement, she revered and honoured Him

as the Creator of the universe, the Eternal
and Almighty God. She saw Him during
His Passion, insulted, outraged, buffeted,
covered with spittle, crowned with thorns,
deserted by His apostles, and condemned to
die on an infamous gibbet between two
malefactors; and yet, with all these indig-
nities and ignominies, Mary recognised
Him as the King of glory, and the Redeemer of mankind. Finally, she beheld
Him dying in agony on the cross, she beheld Him taken down and laid in the tomb;
and still she believed Him immortal, and
that He shall presently rise again full of
life and glory, to subdue the entire universe
to His Gospel and His dominion. Oh Mary,
how great is thy faith! Nothing is capable
of disturbing it, neither the abasement of
a God born in a stable, nor the opprobrium
of His Passion, nor His cruel death on the
cross; thou art superior to every proof, thou
believest unwaveringly despite every trial.
Oh, how does the firmness of thy faith condemn the weakness of ours! But Mary's
faith was not only firm and immovable, it
was also a practical and living faith, she
faithfully observed all the commands of
God. What attention to her prayers! what

recollection in the house of God! what
patience and resignation under trials and
sufferings! what charity towards her neighbour! what tender love for God! what
hatred of sin! what zeal and earnestness in
the fulfilment of every duty!

In such trials and temptations as our
faith may be exposed to, let us call to mind
the constancy and firmness of that of Mary.
Like her, let nothing shake our faith, neither
the difficulties that may present themselves
to our minds, nor the sneers of the ungodly;
let us never be ashamed of our religion and
our title of Christians, for Jesus Christ has
said in His Gospel (Matt. x. 13), "He that
shall deny me before men, I will also deny
him before my Father who is in heaven."
Especially, let us manifest our faith in our
good works and conduct, for it is not enough
for salvation that we have faith. "The
devils believe," says the apostle St. James
(Ep. ii. 19), still they are in hell. To
attain to heaven we must practise as well
as believe. How many Christians shall be
rejected at the last day, not for want of
faith, but for not having practised what
they believed! Of what advantage for us
to believe that there is a hell where souls

suffer unspeakable torments, if we take no
care to avoid it; to believe there is a heaven where those who dwell there are sove-
reignly happy, if we labour not to secure
ourselves the possession of it? Let our life
then be in conformity with our belief;
concerning ourselves seriously about our
salvation ; strictly fulfilling all our duties;
in a word, showing forth our faith in the
practice of good works, without which our
faith will avail us absolutely nothing before
God; or rather it will only serve as our
accuser and will be the means of our greater
condemnation.

EXAMPLE.

Faith rewarded.

A pupil of the seminary of Versailles, named
Peter Renaud, had become, from the effects of very
great bodily sufferings, completely blind. His eye-
lids had shrunk back, leaving exposed the ball of
the eye that was immovable like that of a statue.
The pupil had even become so insensible, that it
could be touched with the finger without causing the
slightest effect. He had, moreover, a disease of the
heart, from which he suffered dreadful agony.
The physicians who attended him declared, that
not only should he never have his sight restored,
but that he should necessarily die of the disease.

For three days and three nights the poor patient endured sufferings that drew from him cries that were heart-rending. Touched by his sad condition, the professors and pupils determined on making in his behalf a novena to the Blessed Virgin, towards whom he entertained a great devotion ; and, accordingly, it was begun on the 4th April, 1845. The following Saturday, the sick person got into a state of extreme weakness, and his malady assumed a most dangerous aspect. He was unconscious, his eyes fixed and wide open, he seemed hardly to breathe. Believing his last moment had come, they hastened to administer to him the sacrament of Extreme Unction. Whilst this was being done, all the community were assembled in the chapel, engaged in earnest prayer for him. About a quarter of an hour after he had been anointed, the patient recovered consciousness, and declared that he no longer was in pain ; he even wished to arise from bed. During the following days he was able to join in most of the public duties of the house. He was cured, but was hopelessly blind. The novena was to end on the 12th April ; he prepared himself by fervent prayer, and confessed and communicated at the community Mass on that morning. God, however, who willed to prove his faith, did not yet restore him to sight ; but, far from losing heart, he continued to pray to the Blessed Virgin, and with redoubled fervour ; he recommended himself to the prayers of the Archconfraternity of Notre Dame des Victoires, and on the 14th April, the second day after the termination of the novena, he determined on approaching again the Holy Communion at the Mass of the community. At the moment of re-

ceiving the adorable Body of Jesus Christ, he heard
a voice that said : " Dost thou believe? Dost thou
believe?" " Yes, Lord, I believe," he replied. " I
believe that Thou canst work a miracle. Thou hast
deprived me of sight; I believe that Thou canst
also restore it to me." His faith was quickly rewarded. On the instant that the consecrated par-
ticle was placed on his tongue, his sight was restored,
and he was able to return to his place without help,
though up to a few moments before he could not
take two steps without being led by the hand. To
test the extent to which his sight was restored to
him, he took up the *Imitation of Christ*, and though
the print was quite small, he read it without difficulty. After Mass, he ran to the sacristy and
cast himself into the arms of the superior, who
could not restrain his tears of joyful surprise.
Great was the enthusiasm, when, during recreation,
he joined his two hundred fellow students, recog-
nising them and addressing them by name. His
poor mother being told of his miraculous cure,
hastened to the seminary to assure herself of it,
but, overcome with emotion, she fainted away.
All these facts occurred in the presence and to the
knowledge of over two hundred witnesses, who can
testify to their accuracy and truth (*Extract from
Report, made to the Bishop of Versailles by the Superior of the Seminary*).

PRACTICE.

Let us ever believe, with firm, undoubting faith,
all the truths of our holy religion; but let us, more-

over, carry them out in practice, for faith without
good works is only a dead faith, that will be of not
the slightest profit to us in gaining heaven.

TWENTY-SIXTH DAY.

FERVENT LOVE OF THE BLESSED VIRGIN FOR GOD.

THE whole life of the Blessed Virgin may
be said to have been one continued act of the
love of God.   From her coming to the use
of reason, as soon as she was capable of
knowing God, she devoted herself to His
service, and loved Him with her whole
heart.   Very different from so many Christians who, after giving to God the years of
early youth, afterwards desert Him for the
sinful pleasures and disorders of the world,
Mary never withdrew from Him.   The
more she advanced in years the more fervently and faithfully did she serve Him.
After the Incarnation of the Eternal Word
in her womb, she increased in fervour and
piety ; her spirit of recollection became
more profound, her prayers more ardent,
her union with God more intimate and per-

fect. But it was particularly after the birth
of Jesus, her Divine Son, that her fervour
and devotion shone forth most brightly.
With what zeal did she consecrate herself
to God her Saviour! with what earnestness
did she devote her life to His service! She
lived and laboured but for Him. What
sufferings did she not endure for His love!
From the moment when she gave Him birth
at Bethlehem to that in which He expired
upon the cross, she never ceased to give
Him proofs of her tender and devoted love.
She shared all His labours, all His sufferings, all His humiliations. In His Passion,
when everyone turned against Him, insulted and outraged Him; when even His
disciples and His apostles deserted, denied,
and abandoned Him, she followed Him to
Calvary, she stood by His cross and watered
it with her tears, and there, too, would she
have died of grief and love if not for a miracle of Providence. After Christ's ascen-
sion into heaven the love of the Blessed
Virgin assumed a new phase, and became
all the more intensified. Unceasingly occupied with the thought of her Divine Son,
her life was a continued prayer and meditation. She dwelt amongst the angels rather

than amongst men. At length, consumed
by the sacred fire with which her soul was
inflamed, she expired, according to sacred
writers, from the effects of her love of God,
and passed to continue in heaven this exercise of charity which had been her happiness and delight upon earth.

If we but loved God as Mary loved Him,
we should find in it our happiness and consolation. And why should we not love a
God who has loved us so much? He loved
us from all eternity, before the world began;
He preserved us by His gifts and graces.
All that we possess, whether in the order
of nature or of grace, comes to us from Him.
Our body with all its members, our soul
with all its faculties, it is He who has conferred them upon us; He it is who pre-
serves, supports, and sustains us. But He
has done far more for us in the order of
grace: He came down from heaven, became
man, suffered the bitterest torments, died
on the cross, and thereon poured out
even to the last drop of His Blood for our
salvation. Not content to have sacrificed
Himself in order to save us, He has also
in His Sacraments left us an inexhaustible
source of graces; He has chosen to remain

Himself amongst us in the adorable Sacrament of the Eucharist, as a Father amidst his children, to be our refuge, our support, and our consolation; and finally, He promises us hereafter eternal happiness in the kingdom of His glory. In return for all these precious favours He asks but one thing only—that we love Him. Oh! should we not be the veriest ingrates were we to withhold from Him our love? Let us, then, love Him with our whole heart, before all things, preferably to all creatures; let us refer all our actions to Him, avoiding all that would displease Him, and be ever disposed to do and suffer all things for His love—in a word, let us faithfully observe all His commandments, for it is in the faithful fulfilment of His holy law that genuine charity consists.

EXAMPLE.

Triumph of Grace.

In the French army sent to Rome after the revolution of 1848, to reinstate the Holy Father in his dominions, there was an officer whose wife was a Protestant. This lady, though brought up in error, was possessed of all the qualities of a good mother. She had two sons, aged ten and twelve years,

whom she carefully trained to virtue. Some days
before the return of the Pope to Rome she desired
to see the apartments prepared for him; and having expressed this desire to her husband, he at
once conducted her to the Vatican Palace, accompanied by her two children. After inspecting the
principal apartments they reached the private
chapel of the Pope. As soon as she entered, perceiving the *prie-dieu* of the Holy Father, she cast
herself on her knees in devotion, and with her
head buried in her hands, poured out a short but
fervent prayer. According to a happy practice
which she had been long accustomed to observe,
although opposed to her religious training, she recommended her two children to the Blessed Virgin;
and having ended her prayer, she raised her eyes
to heaven. But, to her amazement, she beheld over
the altar a lady clad in dazzling white, holding her
two children by the hand, and at the altar the
Pope himself, who seemed to regard her. Struck,
moved to tears by so strange a spectacle, she looked
around to convince herself that her sons were still
at her side. Remarking her emotion, her husband
asked her the cause. "Oh, it is nothing," she replied; "it is only a passing indisposition." The
recollection of the apparition, however, never ceased
to haunt her. On the 12th April following, the
day on which the Pope re-entered Rome, she hastened to the Church of St. John Lateran, where
the Holy Father was to make his first visit. No
sooner did she see Pius IX. than she perfectly recognised every feature. But how much more was
her surprise increased when she saw above him the
same lady whom she had seen at the Vatican, and

who held as before her two children by the hand!
She was so filled with emotion at the sight that
everyone thought her to be taken suddenly ill.
She, however, gradually obtained the mastery over
her feelings, and, as on the former occasion, kept
the occurrence a secret. But a third assault of grace
was reserved for her. Some time afterwards, all
the officers' wives being admitted to an audience by
the Sovereign Pontiff to receive his benediction,
this Protestant lady presented herself, accompanied
by her two sons. Having blessed the children and
given to each a chaplet, the Pope proceeded to
bless the mother, when all at once she was favoured
for the third time with the same miraculous apparition, and with the same attendant circumstances
as on each of the former occasions. This time
she was completely overcome ; she passed the following night in sighs and tears. Finally grace
triumphed in her heart ; she yielded to its salutary
influence, and on the 17th May she solemnly abjured the errors of Protestantism and embraced
the Catholic faith, in which she experienced such
peace and consolation as she had never known before (*Extrait de plusieurs journaux*).

PRACTICE.

Never forget that wo are placed here on earth
but to know, love, and serve God, and that if wo
love Him not in this life we shall burn eternally
in the next. O my God, I desire to fulfil Thy holy
commands !

TWENTY-SEVENTH DAY.

THE BLESSED VIRGIN'S ADMIRABLE CHARITY TOWARDS HER NEIGHBOUR.

THE great love which the Blessed Virgin had for God rendered her exceedingly charitable towards her neighbour; for one cannot truly love God without loving his neighbour, who was formed according to His image and likeness and was ransomed by His Blood. Mary practised this amiable virtue all through her life. Never was she heard to utter a word prejudicial to the character of her neighbour; never did she suffer herself to blame or criticise his conduct; never did she give offence or wound the feelings of any one. Ever affable and mild towards all, she avoided with care all that could give pain to others; she bore with their peculiarities and defects, compassionated their sorrows, consoled them in their afflictions, assisted them in their necessities, and rendered them kind services in every way. Severe towards herself and indulgent towards others, Mary never formed injurious suspicions or rash judgments about her neighbour; she never con-

demned them on slight grounds, on the
contrary, she sought to excuse them; and
if excuse was impossible, she left the matter
in the hands of God, who penetrates the
secrets of hearts, but she judged them not
herself. O admirable conduct! how should
we always study to imitate it, and yet how
rarely do we succeed in doing so!

The charity of Mary was universal and
excepted no one. Persons often deceive
themselves with regard to the fulfilment of
the precept of charity; they flatter themselves they possess this virtue, whilst hatred
and rancour against certain fellow-Christians
lurk at the bottom of their hearts. This is
a fatal delusion. True charity makes no
exception; it requires of us to love all mankind, even our enemies, for God and in
God; to be ready to do good to those who
do us evil, and to pray for those who
hate and persecute us. Mary has also given
us an example of this sublime charity. A
mother can have no more bitter enemies
than those who put to death her only son,
the object of all her affections. Now, on
Calvary, Mary beheld the executioners who
were inflamed with cruel hatred against her
Divine Son, who fastened Him to a cross by

piercing His hands and feet, who shed His
Blood to its last drop, and put Him to death
in the most protracted and cruel manner;
and yet so far from invoking vengeance
and giving expression to her abhorrence of
these inhuman monsters, she prayed for
them, she interceded for them, and begged
of the Eternal Father grace and pardon for
them, saying, like Jesus Christ Himself:
" My God, pardon them, for they know not
what they do." A Mother praying and ask-
ing pardon for the murderers of her Son;
what admirable, what heroic charity !

How far removed from such charity as
that of Mary are we, who have such difficulty in forgetting and pardoning the
slightest offences ! How little does our conduct resemble hers ! Ever indulgent towards
ourselves and severe upon others, we shut
our eyes to our own faults and have them
ever intently fixed upon the defects of others.
So soon as we perceive or fancy that we
detect something censurable in the character
or conduct of our neighbour, we burn with
impatience to make it known; we blame
and criticise him; we impute unworthy
motives to him, entertain injurious suspicions about him, and judge and condemn

him on the slightest grounds. What a severe judgment in consequence shall we
have to undergo when hereafter we shall be
arraigned before the judgment seat of God!
For Jesus Christ has said in His Gospel,
"Judge not, and you shall not be judged.
Condemn not, and you shall not be condemned. . . . For with the same measure that you shall mete withal, it shall be
measured to you again" (Luke, vi. 37, 38).
Let us, then, be ever indulgent towards our
brethren if we would have God so towards
us. Let us never judge and condemn them
lightly and on first appearances. On the
contrary, let us study to surround their acts
with the robe of charity, and God, who is
charity itself, shall deal mercifully with us
when we appear before His tribunal.

EXAMPLE.

The Charitable Soldier.

In the year 1826, a brave soldier, who was in
garrison at Metz, met one day at the corner of the
street a young boy of nine years of age, who was
crying bitterly. "Why do you cry, my child?" he
said. "Oh! I am very unhappy," replied the boy.
"What makes you so?" "Within the last few
days I have lost both my father and mother, and

now I have no one and know not where to go."
The kind-hearted soldier was touched with compassion; so, taking the child by the hand, he brought
him to a place of shelter, and, paying for his support in advance, said to the owner of the house,
"Take care of this child for me, and be kind to
him." Having got the address of the priest of the
place from which the boy said he had come, he
wrote to him at once and received the following reply : "Alas! what the child states is only too true.
He has neither father nor mother. Send him to
us; perhaps we shall be able to find some charitable
soul who will undertake the care of the poor
orphan." The soldier at once replied that he
charged himself with the care of the boy, that he
adopted him, and would do what he could to supply
towards him the place of his lost parents. Having
completed just then his term of service, he re-engaged that very day for a second term, by which he
secured a sum of 1800 francs. Then hastening to
the master of a public school he handed him the
money, saying, "This is to pay for six years the
pension of this child, who is my adopted son ; give
him a good, religious education." He then went to
a church, and prostrating himself before the altar
of the Blessed Virgin, "Holy Virgin," he said "I
consign and consecrate to you my child; take care
of his soul, I will take care of his body; he is
friendless and an orphan, be a mother to him." At
the end of a year the soldier came to see his adopted
child, but alas! what a cruel disappointment! The
boy was reported to him as idle, disorderly, and
vicious. "Take your child," said the superior, "for
I can make nothing of him, and he is upsetting the

whole school." The soldier reflected an instant, grief painted on his countenance and great tears coursing down his cheeks—"O sir," he said, in a voice broken with sobs, "keep him, I beg of you, for six months more; I hope that God will have pity on him and me, and that he will come to be better disposed." The superior consented, and the pious soldier went once more to throw himself at the feet of Mary. "O Blessed Virgin, you forget," he said, with frank, military simplicity, "I entrusted this poor child to you, and asked you to be a mother to him, and yet you leave him to perish! I have sold myself to provide for him, and you are not taking care of his salvation! Oh! once more I implore of you not to forsake him; watch over him, and make him virtuous and dutiful, and I will pray to you and love you always." In the course of another year the soldier returned again. Mary had heard his prayer, the boy had quite reformed, and had even become by the regularity of his conduct a source of edification to all the house. Later on he entered college, and finally had the happiness to become a priest, in which holy state he was a model of piety to his brother priests as he had previously been to his fellow students. Happy child to have met with this charitable soldier! Happy soldier to have fulfilled the offices of charity towards this poor, friendless child (*L'Abbé Connac*).

PRACTICE.

Be always full of charity towards your neighbour. Shun all that would wound his feelings or harm his reputation; bear with his peculiarities

and his defects; readily pardon him any injury he
may do you; render him kind service when the
occasion offers; in a word, do all towards him
that you would have done for yourself, and you
will thus fulfil the precept of Jesus Christ, who
commands us to love our neighbour as ourself.

TWENTY-EIGHTH DAY

VIGILANCE WHICH THE BLESSED VIRGIN EXER-
CISED OVER HERSELF.

ALTHOUGH she was exempt from original
sin and from proclivity to evil, still Mary
exercised a constant and careful vigilance
over herself. She watched over her heart,
her thoughts, words, and actions; she
guarded her senses so as to shun every occasion of sin. Ever prepared against a surprise from the enemy, she trembled at the
slightest danger, distrusted herself and her
own strength, and had recourse to every
means to keep her heart pure and innocent.
Wholly engrossed in the duties of her state
of life, she lived in strict seclusion and recollection; never left home except to visit
the Temple or to discharge the offices of
charity; shunned the world, and frequented
the society only of the wise and virtuous.

She spoke little, and her words were marked
by modesty and reserve; all her conversa-
tion was of heaven. Never was she seen
unoccupied, for she knew that nothing is
more dangerous to virtue than idleness.
When her hands were not employed in work
she gave herself to prayer and the study of
the sacred writings, in which was her chief
happiness and delight. She was as mortified as she was active and laborious; her
moderation and self-denial were unequalled
—it might have been said of her that she
took food only to keep from dying; and in
her choice of food she selected nothing with
a view to gratify the palate, but everything
the simplest and plainest. She gave but
little time to sleep, as much only as was
necessary to recruit her strength. She
never sought to gratify self, but, on the contrary, studied to mortify the flesh, to crucify
and keep it in subjection. She especially
practised interior mortification; bore in a
spirit of penance and for love of God every
trial and affliction that heaven sent her.
Thus did she advance daily more and more
in the way of sanctity and perfection; and
thus did she attain to the high degree of
glory which she now possesses in heaven.

How different our conduct is from that of Mary! "Mary has nothing to fear," says St. Ambrose, "and she fears all things; and we who have everything to fear, fear nothing." Mary had no propensity to evil, and she constantly watched over herself; and we who are so frail and so prone to sin, observe scarcely any precaution—often we even go into occasions and expose ourselves to the danger of sin. Is it, then, to be wondered at that our falls are so frequent and so grievous? Let us, then, watch over ourselves ; over our heart, to root out from it every attachment that is not according to God; over our mind, to repress every evil thought, every culpable desire. Let us keep watch over our eyes, by avoiding all dangerous glances; over our tongue, by never uttering anything that could wound charity or disedify our neighbour; in a word, let us keep guard upon all our senses, for it is through the senses that sin finds entrance into the soul. Let us avoid all dangerous occasions, and frequent the society of those only whose conduct is pious and edifying; let us avoid idleness, as the parent of all vice; finally, let us add prayer to vigilance, according to

the precept of Jesus Christ—"Watch ye, and
pray," He says to us, "that you enter not
into temptation" (Matt. xxvi. 41). By
observing these precautions we shall avoid
sin, we shall persevere in virtue, and shall
secure our eternal salvation.

EXAMPLE.
A Courageous Act.

It was the year 1831, a period when the practice
of religion was but little attended to in the colleges
of Paris, especially in the military school called the
Polytechnic. One of the students in this school
in walking through one of the halls found a beads.
"A beads in the Polytechnic!" he said, picking it
up; "how strange! Is it possible that any one
amongst us recites the beads? Oh! it is incredible
—impossible!" In his opinion it was a disgrace to
recite the beads. He therefore determined to turn
into ridicule the virtuous young man who had remained faithful to Mary. It was the close of the
scholastic year, and each of the pupils was preparing for his examination. The general examination
was presided over by a distinguished man, one of
the veteran marshals of France. Amongst the
students was one who particularly distinguished
himself by the cleverness and knowledge he displayed, and also by his bearing—so full of gravity
and intelligence, but, at the same time, of sweetness and modesty. When the exercises were over,
and before dismissing the pupils, the Marshal had

them put in rank and inspected them in the ordinary playground of the establishment. Towards the conclusion a young man suddenly stepped out from the ranks, and, holding up a beads, cried out in a jeering, insulting tone, "Who has lost the beads? Who is the fool, the booby, that says the beads?" He judged that whoever it was that had dropped the beads would not venture to claim it, and thereby expose himself to the ridicule of his comrades; but hardly had he done speaking when a young man quietly advanced and said, in a firm, collected tone, "The beads is mine; be kind enough to give it me. My mother gave it to me when leaving home for Paris, and I promised her to keep it and recite it whilst I live." The young student who thus spoke was the same who had made such a brilliant examination. The old Marshal advanced to him, and seizing him by the hand, "Young man," he said, "I congratulate you on what you have done; you have shown that you have courage equal to your talent. Be always as ready to defend your religion and you will secure the esteem of every upright man." All the pupils applauded these noble words, and many of them who had been restrained by human respects, feared no longer to practise their religion openly. Let us, like this young man, show ourselves faithful servants of Mary, and she on her part will bless us and bestow abundant favours upon us (*Rosier de Marie*, 12th *June*, 1858).

PRACTICE.

Observe a constant vigilance over yourself, in
order to keep from sin; guard your heart, your
senses, your imagination. Remember that a moment of forgetfulness and incaution may prove
your destruction.

———

TWENTY-NINTH DAY.

INVIOLABLE PURITY OF THE BLESSED
VIRGIN.

PURITY, decorum and modesty, were the
fairest ornaments of the Blessed Virgin. In
her tenderest youth she consecrated herself
to God by a vow of perpetual chastity, and
never did she do aught that in the slightest
degree infringed this solemn engagement.
Purity was ever her privileged virtue. We
can hardly estimate how highly she prized
this angelical virtue, how much she dreaded
anything that should tarnish it, and what
precaution she took to maintain its most
perfect observance. She knew that chastity
is amongst the virtues as the lily is amongst
flowers, that its sensitive delicacy is tar-
nished by the least adverse breath, and,

accordingly, she avoided with the utmost
care all that could affect it with the slightest taint; she shrunk from even the appear-
ance of evil. Thus, at the mere presence
of the angel, she was troubled and alarmed;.
and when the angel proposed to her to become the Mother of the Saviour, she would.
not accept this sublime dignity until she
had received the assurance that her divine
maternity should be nowise incompatible
with her virginal purity. Thus did she
prefer the glory of virginity to that of being
the Mother of God, the Queen of Heaven,
and Sovereign of the universe. What a
love of chastity! Oh! no, none ever loved
this holy virtue as Mary loved it. Virgin
by choice and inclination, it was in chastity
that she centred all her happiness and
delight; Virgin in body and mind, her
thoughts, desires, words, acts, and feelings,
breathed innocence and sanctity; Virgin
before she became a mother, Virgin after
bringing forth her Divine Infant, she was
ever the chastest, the most pure of virgins,.
and so shall be for all eternity. Thus it is
the Church styles her the Holy, the Blessed
Virgin, the Virgin by excellence, and the
Queen of Virgins; and even when address-

ing her by her title of Mother of God, she
still adds that of Virgin, because she knows
full well that nothing is more pleasing to
Mary than that august quality. It is, in
truth, her brightest crown and her most
glorious title.

But if the Church so frequently reminds
us of the inviolable purity of Mary, it is
not only that we may admire this sweet
virtue, but, yet more, that we may be
induced to practise it. Whatever be our
state and condition in life, we are all bound
to be chaste and pure. Jesus Christ has
imposed it upon us by a formal and rigorous
precept; and not only does He forbid all
acts that are contrary to purity, but also all
thoughts and desires that would wound
this angelical virtue. St. Paul forbids even
the naming of the opposite vice amongst
Christians, to show us how abominable it
is in the eyes of God. There are few crimes
that God has more severely punished than
this, even in this life. We have terrible
examples of this fact recorded in the Sacred
Scriptures, where we find Him never allow-
it to go unpunished. But it is in the next
life that He will most severely deal with
it. It is there that He shall pour out all

the vials of His wrath on those who have
given themselves up to this shameful vice;
there shall they be plunged in a sea, an
ocean of fire, from which they shall never
escape. Let us, therefore, avoid with care
all that would tend to draw us into this
accursed sin. Think not that you can be
too careful on this point, you cannot be
enough so. Let us watch over our thoughts,
our words, our attachments; let us keep
guard over all our senses, that there may be
never anything in us contrary to purity;
let us frequent the sacraments of Penance
and the Blessed Eucharist; let us practise
sobriety and mortification; let us fly all
dangerous occasions, for were we even
saints and angels of purity, if we expose
ourselves to danger we shall infallibly perish in it; the word of God says so. Finally,
let us have recourse to prayer, saying often
with the holy king David: Create in me, O
Lord, a right spirit, a pure heart, a heart
ever disposed to fulfil Thy holy law.

EXAMPLE.
A Fate and a Warning.

In 1604, in one of the Flemish cities, there were
two young students, who, instead of applying them-

selves to their studies, abandoned themselves to an
irregular and licentious life. One evening, when
they were together as usual in some of their haunts
of crime, one of them, named Richard, begged his
companion to come away, and when he refused,
Richard left and returned home alone. As he prepared for bed, he recollected that he had not yet
recited certain Hail Marys which he had, notwithstanding his evil courses, been hitherto faithful in
repeating every day. He was so overcome with
sleep, he found the utmost difficulty in going through
his customary prayers. Having, however, somehow
repeated them, he lay down and fell asleep. But,
almost on the moment, he was awakened by his
door being shaken violently. He sat up in bed, and
listened. Presently the door opened, and he saw
his companion enter, pale, disfigured, like a spectre,
who advanced towards him, and said: "Richard,
do you know me?" "What!" replied Richard, "is
it you, my friend? But what is amiss. You frighten
me. Is it a joke that you are playing?" "Ah! woe's
me!" cried the poor wretch; "the time for joking is
past. I am damned, and for ever. In leaving the
scene of our crimes, I was struck with a sudden
death; my body lies in the street, and my soul is
buried in hell. The same fate was to have been
yours; you were included in the same sentence; but
Mary took you under her protection in return for
the poor honour you used to pay to her. Happy
will you be if you take advantage of the warning
which she has given you to-day." Pronouncing
these words, the spectre disappeared. Richard,
half dead with fright, cast himself on the floor, and
with his face to the earth, fervently thanked his

protectress. Whilst considering what he should do
in changing his life, he heard the bell sounding for
matins at the Franciscan Monastery. At once his
resolution was taken. "Thither it is," he said,
"that God calls me." He went forthwith to the
convent and asked to be received. The monks, who
had heard of his disorderly life, refused him
admittance, but, on hearing what had happened
during the night, they consented to receive him.
Two of the religious went to the place indicated to
ascertain the truth of his statement, and there, in
fact, they found the corpse of his unfortunate companion, stretched in the street. As to Richard, he
was received into the community, and there became
a model of every virtue. In the end, he went to
the Indies to bear thither the faith of Jesus Christ,
and from thence to Japan, where he ended his life
by a glorious martyrdom (*Glories of Mary: St.
Liguori*).

PRACTICE.

Entertain a sovereign horror of the sin of impurity. Have recourse to every precaution to
preserve yourself free from this accursed vice
you cannot be too careful in avoiding a sin so
abominable in the eyes of God, a sin that sends
millions of souls to hell.

THIRTIETH DAY.

THE TRIALS AND SUFFERINGS OF THE BLESSED VIRGIN.

NEXT to Jesus Christ, no one ever underwent so much of earthly suffering as the Blessed Virgin. Her entire life was but a continual succession of afflictions, trials, and sacrifices. At Nazareth, at Bethlehem, in Egypt, in each and every place, she met with the severest trials, and the bitterest and most poignant sorrows. Jesus, who so often wrought miracles for the relief of the unhappy, never did so to avert sufferings from His holy Mother. On the contrary, it might be said that events were so disposed as that she might have the more to suffer; never was she relieved of her cross; God willed that her life should be a long and painful martyrdom. Why did Jesus assign this lot to His Divine Mother? Oh! it was because He loved her with an infinite love that He thus subjected her to those severe trials; it was because He would elevate her in glory above the angels and saints that He permitted these accumulated

sorrows and afflictions to come upon her.
It is thus God treats the souls whom He
most dearly loves; He proves them severely
in this life, in order to recompense them
generously for ever hereafter.

But the keenest and most painful of all
the dolours of Mary was that which she
experienced on Calvary at the death of her
Divine Son. There she had before her the
most overwhelming spectacle that could
present itself to the eyes of a mother. She
beheld her beloved Son extended, nailed on
a cross; she saw Him all over bruised,
bloody, and disfigured, His brow crowned
with thorns, His sacred face covered with
spittle, His hands and feet transpierced,
His whole body, from the sole of His feet
to the top of His head, showing one con-
tinuous and ghastly wound. For three hours
she had this heartrending spectacle before
her eyes. Her soul was bowed down in
anguish, deluged with grief, and yet not
one word of murmur or complaint escaped
her lips, no feeling of anger or impatience
arose in her heart; her perfect submission
and conformity to the will of God rendered
her mute and wholly resigned.

Alas! how far are we from copying after

the patience and resignation of the Blessed
Virgin! So soon as we have anything to
suffer, we forthwith complain and murmur
and become impatient, and thus we lose the
fruit of our trials and our sufferings. Yet,
we must endure trials if we would gain
heaven. The Holy Scripture tells us that
it is through many tribulations we are to
enter into the kingdom of God. Therefore,
the greatest saints are those who have suffered most, and been the most severely
proved. Besides, we shall never have as
much to suffer as we deserve. Had we
committed but one mortal sin during our life,
we merited to suffer for it eternally in hell.
When that is so, how can we repine and
think our lot too hard if we have to suffer
for a few years in this life? Instead, then,
of murmuring and complaining, let us support with patience and resignation all such
afflictions as God in His mercy sends us.
Let us unite our sorrows and crosses to
those which Jesus Christ endured for us,
and thus render them meritorious. Let us,
also, offer to God, in penance for our sins,
all the little trials and annoyances which we
meet with nearly every day, such as illness,
contradictions, cutting words, the disagree-

able ways of those with whom we have to live, the inconveniences of heat and cold, and the like. Such things as these, borne in patience, and for love of God, afford to us opportunities of meriting much for heaven, and means of expiating and making satisfaction for our sins to the Divine Justice. "Oh! how sweet it is to suffer," says St. Bernard, "when by it, we merit a happiness that shall endure for ever, and we escape the sufferings that shall never end!"

EXAMPLE.

Heroic resignation of a Christian Mother.

Monsignor Pellerin, Vicar Apostolic in northern Cochin China, relates a deed of heroism worthy the first ages of the Church. A cruel persecution, that for several years had deluged that unhappy country with blood, still raged in all its fury. A woman, advanced in life, had an only son; he was the sole comfort and support of her declining years. This son, in whom all her affections centred, was about to be arrested and put to death as a Christian. The despairing mother came to cast herself at the feet of the missioner; her cries were heartrending. The words of the missioner, exhorting her to resignation, were at first in vain; nothing could comfort her or assuage her grief. At last he reminded her of the example of Mary. He told her that Mary also had an only Son, whom she loved as never before had mother loved a child, still she followed Him to Calvary and witnessed His death without uttering a complaint, although He was condemned unjustly, and saw Him die amidst the cruelest agonies. Strengthened by these words, the woman stood up, her cries ceased, and her tears no longer flowed. Her heart was full of sorrow, but she bore it in silence; she became submissive and resigned. Presently the merciless executioners came to seize their prey and to drag him to death: she followed. Arrived at the fatal spot, the young man was put upon his knees, and the headsman brandished his sword; the mother advanced, and holding up a portion of her dress, without uttering a word of complaint, received into it the bleeding head of her martyred child; then bearing this precious treasure she returned to the missioner to show him how she had followed the example of Mary; but borne down by her emotions, stricken by the weight of her sorrows, she fell senseless at the feet of the minister of God, who knew not which the most to admire, the heroic courage or the holy resignation of this virtuous mother (*Couronne de Marie*).

PRACTICE.

Never forget that suffering is the portion of the elect, and that to go to heaven we must pass through trials and tribulations. Oh! if the most holy and most perfect of creatures, if the Mother of God has suffered so much, how shall we dare to complain, when we, who are guilty sinners, have something to suffer?

THIRTY-FIRST DAY.

Two things should enlist our confidence :
the power and the will to do us good. Now
the Blessed Virgin unites these two qualities in an eminent degree. She is all-
powerful in heaven, she is full of mercy
towards us. Mary is Mother of God,
Mother of Jesus Christ, and by reason of
that title, she enjoys the utmost influence
over the Heart of her Divine Son; Jesus
can refuse her nothing. Trace our adorable
Saviour through all the recorded acts of
His life, and you shall find that He ever
regarded it as a duty to obey His holy
Mother and to fulfil her wishes.

If Mary already possessed such power
with her Divine Son, whilst yet on earth,
whilst yet a poor, feeble, mortal woman,.
how limitless must be her power now that
she is in heaven, now that Jesus has seated
her at the right of His throne of glory, now
that she has been crowned the Queen of
angels and saints, and has been constituted.

the Depository of His graces and treasures? Hence, the Fathers and Doctors of the Church have not hesitated to affirm that Mary is all-powerful in heaven and on earth, that she is the sovereign Dispensatrix of God's graces, and that they are conveyed through her to us, in such measure as she wills to bestow them.

But Mary is not only all-powerful in heaven, she is also full of pity and love for us; for she is our Mother, and we are her children. Now, we know full well how a mother loves her children; that she loves them more than herself, more than life. How often have we known mothers to face the greatest dangers, to expose themselves to risk of death, in order to snatch their offspring from impending peril? But Mary has done much more for us than this. Mary had one only Son; He was the most amiable and perfect of the children of men; He was God. She loved Him more tenderly than ever before or since did mother love her child; she would have undergone death a thousand times to save His life, and yet she consents through love of us that He should die. Yes, on Calvary, the maternal heart of Mary was divided between

two loves—her love for her Divine Son and
her love for us.   She had to choose between
these two; either to yield up her Jesus to
die on the cross a most cruel death, or to
leave us to perish eternally, and Mary did
not hesitate ; she resigned her Jesus into
the hands of the executioners, to undergo
an agonizing death, that we might be saved.
But if such was Mary's tender love for
us whilst still on earth, as to sacrifice her
Son for love of us, how much greater is her
love for us now that she is in the possession
of glory, in the abode of perfect love; now
that she knows so much more our miseries
and our needs ; now that she is so powerful
with God and can so readily aid and help us!
    Have, therefore, confidence in Mary; let
your trust in her be unbounded, universal,
tender, and childlike; in all your needs,
whether corporal or spiritual, whether for
yourself or for others, have recourse to
this sweet Mother, to this powerful Protectress; she will hasten to your assistance,
she will console you in your sorrows, soften
your afflictions, help you in dangers, and
defend you against temptations.   The
more unhappy and unfortunate we are the
more will she interest herself about us, for

a mother never is more anxious about her
children than when she sees them in want
and trouble. Let us consecrate ourselves
entirely and for ever to her service; let us
allow no day to pass without praying to
her; let us especially labour to acquire the
virtues of which she sets us the example;
and how violent soever be our passions, how
frequent our relapses, whatever, or how
great soever be the difficulties in the way
of our salvation, we shall succeed in saving
our souls with Mary's help; for it has
never yet been heard that any one was lost
who was under the protection of this sweet
Mother.

EXAMPLE.

Tender confidence in Mary.

In 1638, a young man of nineteen named Michael
Pellicer, a native of Arragon in Spain, fell from a
cart loaded with corn; the wheel passed over the
left leg and broke it. His parents being very poor,
he was conveyed to the great hospital of Saragossa,
there to receive medical treatment; but before
entering, he begged to be brought to the subterra-
nean chapel, where a statue of the Blessed Virgin
is very specially honoured, under the title of Our
Lady of the Pillar. In dreadful pain though he
was, he confessed, heard Mass, and received Holy

Communion; after which, with a resigned heart, he
allowed himself to be carried to the hospital, and
yielded himself up to the care of the physician. The
doctor, on seeing the state of the limb, at once declared that there was nothing for it but amputation.
The leg was accordingly cut off below the knee, and
the amputated limb was buried. During the painful operation, the patient uttered no complaint;
but he never ceased invoking the Blessed Virgin,
in whom he had the most tender confidence. When
the wound was healed, he crawled upon crutches
to the feet of Our Lady of the Pillar to thank her
for the strength she had obtained for him when
undergoing the operation. After some time, the
wound being entirely healed, Michael Pellicer
returned home to his parents less a limb, but ever
entertaining a most lively confidence in Mary.
One evening, after a day spent in going through
the neighbouring villages begging alms, quite tired
out, he went to bed, leaving his wooden leg beside
the fire-place, where his father and mother sat.
After some time his mother, anxious lest his
fatigue had made him unwell, came into his little
room to see if he slept. What was her astonishment to see two feet in place of one! She ran to
tell her husband. He quickly awakened his son,
who, opening his eyes, exclaimed: "Ah! why have
you awakened me out of such a delightful dream?
I dreamt that I was in the chapel of Our Lady of
the Pillar, and that, in recompense for the confidence which I always had in her, she had my lost
limb replaced by two angels." "It is not a dream,"
replied his father, "for your limb is in truth
restored." Their cries of joy, drew their neigh-

hours around them; the fame of this wonderful miracle soon spread abroad, and great numbers came to witness it. The leg was perfectly restored; there only remained a red mark showing where it had been amputated, a mark that never disappeared. This miracle, established by the most incontestable and convincing proofs, was publicly admitted and proclaimed by the Archbishop of Saragossa, on the 16th April, 1641 (*Bollandists, 25th July*).

THE END.

www.ingramcontent.com/pod-product-compliance
Lightning Source LLC
Chambersburg PA
CBHW030845270326
41928CB00007B/1230